writers
and their times

F. Scott Fitzgerald

and the
Jazz Age

Alison Morretta

Cavendish
Square

New York

For Bart

Published in 2015 by Cavendish Square Publishing, LLC
243 5th Avenue, Suite 136, New York, NY 10016

Library of Congress Cataloging-in-Publication Data

Morretta, Alison.
F. Scott Fitzgerald and the Jazz Age / Alison Morretta.
pages cm. — (Writers and their times)
Includes bibliographical references and index.
ISBN 978-1-62712-815-5 (hardcover) ISBN 978-1-62712-817-9 (ebook)
1. Fitzgerald, F. Scott (Francis Scott), 1896-1940—Criticism and interpretation. 2. United States—History—1919-1933.
Nineteen twenties. I. Title.

PS3511.I9Z735 2015
813'.52—dc23

2014003728

Editorial Director: Dean Miller   Designer: Amy Greenan
Editor: Kristen Susienka   Production Manager: Jennifer Ryder-Talbot
Senior Copy Editor: Wendy A. Reynolds   Production Editor: David McNamara
Art Director: Jeffrey Talbot   Photo Research: J8 Media

Contents

Introduction

Booms and Busts

The story of F. Scott Fitzgerald is the story of Jazz Age America. A member of "The Lost Generation" that came of age during World War I, Fitzgerald's rapid rise and fall mirrored the boom and bust of the Roaring Twenties. Where some men invested their life savings in the stock market, Fitzgerald invested everything in his work and his wife, Zelda. Both had disastrous consequences.

Fitzgerald was both a chronicler and a critic of Jazz Age culture. He spent his youth aspiring to fame and success, which he achieved at a very young age with the publication of his first novel, *This Side of Paradise*, in 1920. The publication of his novel coincided with the beginning of the Roaring Twenties, and the possibilities of the new decade seemed endless for the young author. However, though he enjoyed the lifestyle that accompanied his newfound celebrity, he remained critical of the Jazz Age culture of excess. His traditional Midwestern values stood in stark contrast to the new American Dream of fame and fortune, and he saw the nation in a state of moral decline.

Uniformed bartenders serve alcohol to customers in a New York City speakeasy in 1933, shortly before the repeal of Prohibition.

His work is a testament to his conflicting attitudes about the time he lived in.

The Jazz Age was a time of great change in American culture. A booming economy gave the impression that money was there for the taking. The ban on alcohol during **Prohibition** made millionaires out of criminals. The modern woman emerged as a cultural symbol and attitudes toward sexuality and gender roles were changing. It was in this environment that Fitzgerald came of age, and his work can be read as both a social history of his time and a critique of it.

While Fitzgerald became famous for his realistic portrayal of Jazz Age culture, he also became an alcoholic. Despite his literary success, he always found himself in need of money, and he came to further resent the culture that valued wealth and success above all things. Fitzgerald's own pursuit of the new American Dream left him broke and in poor health, and by the

PANTAGES SWINGS MOP.—Dejected at conviction on assault charge by Eunice Pringle, 17, Alexander Pantages (with cigar), theatrical magnate, is forced to mop up like other prisoners while awaiting sentence in Los Angeles jail. He is unable to eat prison fare. Here he is entering jail with deputy sheriffs. —*Story on page 37.*

CLOUDS HAD GOLDEN LINING.— Mrs. Edith Murphy Belpasi Healy (above), came back from west yesterday with Reno divorce from Percy C. Healy, wealthy broker, and $500,000 alimony. Healy wooed her in plane. —*Story on page 16.*

SUSPICIOUS $250,000 FIRE.—Flames that shot high above roof of six-story apartment house nearing completion in West 183d st. yesterday provided thrilling spectacle. Damage was $250,000. Police seek disgruntled former employe who left building before fire. —*Story on page 16; other pics, p. 24.*

"OOH LA LA!"—Irene Bordoni seems to be getting some exciting news over phone. Maybe it's about the suit she filed in Chicago yesterday for annulment of marriage to E. Ray Goetz, producer. She charges she was never really married to Goetz because he married her less than a year after he'd divorced Ethel Johnson Goetz. —*Story on page 5.*

Headline of the "Black Tuesday" issue of the *New York Daily News* announces the collapse of the New York Stock Exchange on October 29, 1929.

Homeless migrant farmers in tent communities called "Hoovervilles" while looking for work in the pea fields of California during the Great Depression, circa 1935.

time of the Great Stock Market Crash in 1929, his career and his life were in shambles.

As America entered the Depression years, Fitzgerald's life followed a similar trajectory. The lighthearted flapper stories that sold so well during the boom times were not marketable during the Great Depression, and the 1930s saw him making very little progress on his work. His marriage had fallen apart, his health was failing, and he was in a great deal of debt. His literary reputation was in ruins, tarnished by his own excess. Much like the nation itself, he had cracked up.

Fitzgerald's life was cut short when he died of a heart attack in 1940. He did not live to see the country come out of the Depression, nor did he live to see the resurgence in the popularity of his work. In "The Author's Apology" (1920), Fitzgerald wrote, "My whole theory of writing I can sum up in one sentence: An author ought to write for the youth of his own generation, the critics of the next, and the schoolmasters of ever afterward." Although written in the very early days of his fame, this prescient statement rings true. Today, *The Great Gatsby* is considered one of the great American novels and remains one of the most widely studied books in the world.

Bee Jackson, world champion of the popular dance style called the Charleston, performs the dance in front of a mirror in 1925.

ONE

From the Great War to the Great Crash

The 1920s in America are commonly referred to as "the Jazz Age," a phrase popularized by F. Scott Fitzgerald to describe the decadent years of prosperity, consumption, and leisure captured in his novels and short stories. The popular image of the Jazz Age is of **flappers** dancing the Charleston in **speakeasies**, **bootlegging** gangsters catering to a nation that rejected Prohibition, and perhaps most importantly, a time when the American Dream of opportunity and wealth was there for the taking. This image, however, is very misleading; in reality, this was a time of major cultural conflict on a national scale.

All the changes taking place in American society at this time—political, social, cultural, and economic—emerged during wartime and in the postwar years immediately preceding the decade known as the Roaring Twenties. It is more accurate then to define the Jazz Age not by decade, but as the years between World War I and the Stock Market Crash of 1929.

U.S. servicemen from the 2nd Pioneer Infantry arrive in Hoboken, New Jersey, after the end of World War I, circa 1918.

The Death of Progressivism

The United States entered World War I on April 6, 1917, with President Woodrow Wilson as its Commander-in-Chief. A **progressive** Democrat, Wilson saw U.S. involvement in the war as a crusade for democracy abroad. However, widespread violations of civil liberties began a pattern of discrimination and conformity at home in America that would continue in the postwar years and flourish during the 1920s.

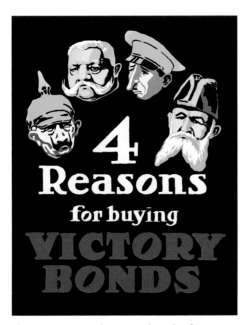

This WWI poster advertising the sale of government bonds, which features caricatured images of the four leaders of the Central Powers.

While American soldiers were fighting for democracy in Europe, their sacrifice was undermined by a pattern of intolerance at home that served as a prelude to widespread anti-immigrant sentiment and legislation in the 1920s. Influenced by government-produced war **propaganda**, Americans grew hostile to the German immigrant population, and German-Americans were subject to discrimination as many questioned their loyalty to the Allied forces. The 1917 October Revolution (during which **Communist** forces known as the **Bolsheviks** overthrew the Russian government) fueled the anti-German sentiment even further, since many Americans believed that the Germans were involved. The wartime Espionage Act (1917) and Sedition Act (1918) gave the U.S. government the authority to arrest individuals who opposed the war and ban antiwar publications from the mail.

Immigration Legislation

A large number of immigrants arrived in America between mid-1920 and early 1921, and with the nativist attitude of the general public and the postwar depression, they were not welcome. To restrict immigration, the Emergency Immigration Act of 1921 used a quota system which favored what were called "old-stock" immigrants (from northern Europe) over

Jazz Age Presidents

Warren G. Harding (1865–1923)

Republican Warren Gamaliel Harding took office as the twenty-ninth President of the United States on March 4, 1921. Previously an Ohio state senator, lieutenant governor, and U.S. senator, Harding ran on a platform promising a return to "normalcy" and "triumphant nationality"–things that appealed to the American public after the war–but his presidency was marred by scandal. Harding engaged in extramarital affairs, gambled, and indulged in bootleg liquor in the White House. He also appointed his friends to cabinet positions.

Despite the scandals, Harding did manage to bring the U.S. out of the **recession** and decrease unemployment. He also fulfilled the promises of his America First program and tightly restricted immigration. His health, however, deteriorated. During a speaking tour, he fell gravely ill and died of a heart attack in San Francisco on August 2, 1923 while still in office. Harding was succeeded by his vice president, Calvin Coolidge.

Calvin Coolidge (1872–1933)

Awakened with the news of Harding's death, John Calvin Coolidge was sworn in as the thirtieth President of the United States at his family home in rural Plymouth Notch, Vermont, on August 3, 1923.

Known as "Silent Cal," Coolidge did not drink or gamble, remained faithful to his wife, and surrounded himself with people with an equally strong moral fiber. Of the opinion that "the chief business of the American people is business," he cut federal spending to reduce debt, lowered income tax rates, and placed pro-business people on regulatory commissions to ensure cooperation between business and government. Coolidge continued his predecessor's policies of **nativism**, further restricting immigration by signing the Immigration Act of 1924.

The boom times of the Roaring Twenties and the scandal-free nature of his presidency gave Coolidge a high approval rating, so it came as a shock when he chose not to run for reelection in the 1928 presidential campaign. He retired to Northampton, where he died of a heart attack on January 5, 1933.

the newer, less desirable immigrants from southern and eastern Europe.

Some people were not satisfied with the 1921 law, however. In 1924, the Johnson-Reed Act (also known as the Immigration Act of 1924) lowered the number of available visas even further. It also banned all immigrants from Asia, which contributed to existing tension between the U.S. and Japan. America lost its reputation as a refuge for the oppressed peoples of the world.

Immigrants are served a beverage after arriving at the processing station on Ellis Island in Upper New York Bay, New York City, in 1920.

New York City Deputy Police Commissioner John A. Leach (right) oversees the disposal of illegal alcohol seized by Prohibition agents after a raid.

Prohibition

There is perhaps nothing more closely associated with the Jazz Age than Prohibition, the nationwide ban on the production, transport, and sale of alcoholic beverages. The Eighteenth Amendment, which went into effect on January 16, 1920, made Prohibition a federal law, but the origins of the temperance movement has its roots in the nineteenth century.

Groups such as the American Temperance Society (ATS), the Women's Christian Temperance Union (WTCU), and later, the Anti-Saloon League (ASL) were mostly made up of middle-class Protestants who believed that drinking created a threat to the nation's spiritual health. They had many supporters: women who believed that outlawing liquor would restore order to the home; business leaders who believed that drinking led to decreased productivity and accidents; white southerners who believed that alcohol consumption by African Americans was dangerous; and progressive reformers who believed that a ban on liquor would eliminate urban poverty and improve the nation's quality of life. America's participation in the war was also a factor—many of America's brewers were of German descent, and widespread anti-German feelings increased support for the cause. By the time the Eighteenth Amendment was ratified on January 16, 1919, many states had already adopted Prohibition laws.

Prohibition Becomes Law

Congress then passed the Volstead Act on October 28, 1919, which defined the "intoxicating liquors" banned by the Eighteenth Amendment as any beverage containing more than 0.5 percent alcohol, and also established the penalties for violating Prohibition laws. Neither the Volstead Act nor the Eighteenth Amendment outlawed the possession or consumption of alcohol, which made it completely legal for people and businesses to store up alcohol before the country went dry. This loophole only benefited the upper class, however, since only they had enough money to be able to purchase alcohol in vast quantities. Other loopholes included an exemption for alcohol used for religious purposes, the medicinal use of alcohol (which many doctors abused by writing unnecessary prescriptions), and an allowance for breweries to produce legal non-alcoholic beer that could easily be fermented after sale.

Bootlegging and Organized Crime

Speakeasies were illegal drinking establishments that provided an alternative to the saloon. Bootleggers, the people who made and/or sold illegal liquor, supplied the alcohol. Not all bootlegging operations were linked with organized crime— some people, especially in the rural south, made their own

Notorious Chicago gangster Al Capone, leader of a successful bootlegging operation during the Prohibition era, poses for a photograph in 1932.

"bathtub gin" in stills on their property and sold it in small quantities. The market in urban areas was too large for this sort of production, however, and organized crime flourished in the cities, particularly in Chicago, during the 1920s.

Without the resources or the manpower to police the U.S. borders and coastline, many local police and federal agents frequently took bribes from bootleggers to look the other way.

17

However, Prohibition violations were not limited to organized crime syndicates and low-level officials. Corrupt members of President Harding's cabinet (known as the "Ohio Gang"), including Attorney General Harry Daugherty, routinely accepted bribes from bootleggers in exchange for pardons, paroles, or protection.

Although alcohol consumption actually decreased during the Prohibition era, the lack of popular support, coupled with the loss of jobs and tax revenue from alcohol production and sales, made its repeal important during the Great Depression. The Twenty-First Amendment, repealing Prohibition, was ratified on December 5, 1933, and the "noble experiment" that had shaped Jazz Age culture and politics officially came to an end.

Secularization of America

While the horrors of World War I had disillusioned many veterans, the decline of traditional religious values, or secularization, of Jazz Age America can be attributed mostly to the major cultural changes of the period. Scientific advances, especially in the fields of biology and psychology, challenged traditional religious beliefs. As people became more materialistic, the increasing rejection of traditional values deeply disturbed some Americans and led to the revival of the Ku Klux Klan (KKK).

Originally formed as a white supremacist group in the post-Civil War South, KKK activity had declined since the Reconstruction era, but the 1920s saw a revival in Klan activity. The second Klan was founded in 1915, but it did not gain much momentum until 1920, when Klan leader William Simmons enlisted two public relations specialists. Taking advantage of prevailing racist and nativist postwar attitudes, they used advertising techniques to rebrand the Klan as "100% American." The Klan achieved some political success in the early 1920s, but several scandals involving Klan leaders ruined its reputation as an

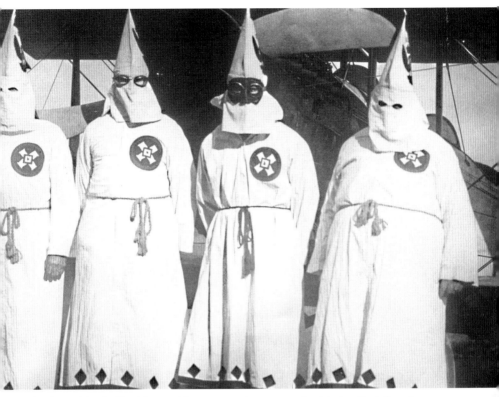

Members of the Ku Klux Klan, a white supremacist group revived during the influx of immigrants in the 1920s, stand in traditional robes and hoods in front of an airplane used to drop propaganda leaflets over the city of Washington, D.C. in 1922.

organization based on traditional morality. Many members lost their enthusiasm for the cause, accepting Jazz Age modernization and Prohibition violations as things they could not change. By the end of the decade, the new Klan had no political power and fewer than 50,000 members across the nation.

The Great Migration

During World War I, the need for unskilled laborers drove many African Americans to seek employment and a better life in the northern cities. The end of the war, however, proved a rude awakening: as white soldiers returned, African Americans were laid off to provide them with jobs. Black veterans returned home to a country that did not recognize or appreciate their

Two young women walk down the beach in Atlantic City, New Jersey, dressed in the typical flapper style, circa 1924.

Residents of the thriving African American community of Harlem in New York City gather on the street outside a luncheonette, circa 1920.

service. Housing discrimination caused tension, forcing the creation of all-black communities such as Harlem in New York City and the Black Belt in Chicago's South Side. Race riots broke out across the nation. Empowered by wartime service and the promise of new opportunity, African Americans became more militant and unified in defending their rights.

The Birth of the "New Woman"

The flapper—with her boyish figure, red lipstick, and short bobbed hair—is one of the most enduring images of Jazz Age culture. Energetic, free-spirited, rebellious, and outspoken, the flapper symbolized a larger change in society: the shift away from the traditional Victorian female to the liberated "New Woman."

21

This "New Woman" drank and smoked in public, danced in speakeasies, and socialized with men without a chaperone—which often lead to mild sexual exploration known as "petting."

Flappers represented an entire shift in gender roles in America, beginning with the Nineteenth Amendment in 1920, which granted women the right to vote. Single women also began working outside the home—often as office workers—and while they usually stopped working after marriage, they enjoyed a greater sense of freedom than their mothers had. This generation gap caused some conflict, as the older generation did not approve of the liberated "New Woman."

Mass Production and the Rise of the Automobile

The introduction of the moving assembly line, perfected by Henry Ford in 1913, made manufacturing automobiles and other goods easier and more profitable. Ford's system, where unskilled laborers stood in place in front of a conveyor belt and worked on one piece of the car as it moved down the line, made production easy, fast, and cheap. The Ford Motor Company used this method to produce the Model T, the first automobile that was affordable enough for the average middle-class family. Not to be outdone, Ford's rival, the General Motors Company (GM), then introduced the idea of consumer credit financed directly by the manufacturer, which enabled buyers to purchase a car without having to pay all the money up front or secure a loan from a bank. By 1920, millions of Americans owned their own automobile.

Leisure Activity

Many Jazz Age employees had shorter hours, higher wages, and weekends free, and some even had paid vacation time. Electricity in the home and the mass production of radios

Employees of the Ford Motor Company's River Rouge factory in Dearborn, Michigan, manufacture Model A automobiles on a moving assembly line in 1927.

made it easy for people, especially in rural areas, to enjoy music, news, drama, comedy, and sports broadcasts from the comfort of their living rooms. The phonograph, or record player, brought jazz and blues to the masses. Of all the leisure activities during this period, the motion picture industry had the most significant effect on American culture.

The 1920s were also considered the golden age of sports, with many people using their leisure time to attend professional sporting events, especially baseball. America's national pastime had been tainted when the 1919 World Series was fixed by gamblers (including notorious bootlegger Arnold Rothstein). Power hitter Babe Ruth revived the sport, setting home run records and becoming a national figure. Newspaper publicity and sports broadcasts on the radio also made celebrities out of

From Silent Films to Talkies

In the early 1920s, silent films were the most popular form of entertainment in America's cities and large towns, and automobiles made it possible for people who lived within driving distance to go to the cinema. Films with synchronized sound, or "talkies," emerged later in the decade. The first feature-length talking picture, *The Jazz Singer*, premiered in 1927 and starred Al Jolson as a man who was torn between his dream of becoming a jazz musician and his traditional Jewish upbringing. The film's main theme—the conflict between traditional and modern values—is something that spoke to many Americans during this period of cultural change.

Designed by Thomas W. Lamb, the lavishly decorated interior of the United Palace Theater in New York City is just one example of the many opulent "movie palaces" that sprung up in America's major cities with the growing popularity of film.

New York Yankee outfielder Babe Ruth, famous for his power hitting and record-shattering number of home runs, poses for a photograph with two young fans, circa 1920s.

boxer Jack Dempsey, football star Knute Rockne, tennis player Helen Wills, and swimmer Gertrude Ederle. The greatest hero of the era was aviator Charles Lindbergh, who became the first person to successfully complete a solo transatlantic flight in May 1927.

President Herbert Hoover (1877–1964)

Herbert Clark Hoover took office as the thirty-first president of the United States on March 4, 1929, just a few months before the Wall Street Crash that signaled the end of the Jazz Age and the start of the Great Depression. As the 1928 Republican presidential candidate when Coolidge chose not to run for reelection, Hoover promised the American people a "final triumph over poverty." However, within eight months of taking office, the economy collapsed. Hoover's inability to bring the nation out of the Depression tarnished his reputation, and he lost his 1932 reelection bid to Democrat Franklin Delano Roosevelt.

Jazz Age Booms and Busts

From 1919 to 1921, the nation experienced a brief period of economic recession that is largely overshadowed by the boom that characterized the decade. The government had amassed huge debts during the war, and when it ended they were forced to cut spending. The returning troops increased the labor force, which led to higher rates of unemployment and lower wages. The demand for production declined sharply, leaving a surplus of goods and no one to buy them.

The **laissez-faire** economic policy of the Republican presidents helped the growth of American business. This approach enabled private corporations to operate with minimal government regulation and turn large profits. Meanwhile, the introduction of credit and installment buying allowed average Americans to purchase cars, radios, and other home appliances that they would not have been able to afford otherwise. The availability of mortgages from banks made the dream of home ownership a reality. The economy recovered, and people began to feel that the American Dream was finally within reach.

With stock prices growing ever higher throughout the second half of the 1920s and no end in sight, many Americans invested their entire savings in the stock market—and some even borrowed money to invest. This type of investment, called buying on margin, was risky. The investor would be issued a **margin call** if the stock price fell, which required the borrower to pay back part, or all, of the loan amount immediately. Banks also took risks by investing their customers' money, believing that profits were assured. In reality, stock prices had exceeded their real value, and with production in decline and unemployment on the rise, disaster was imminent.

October 29, 1929, known as "Black Tuesday," is considered the worst day in the history of the New York Stock Exchange. Prices plummeted, margin calls were issued, and even the

The headline of the *Brooklyn Daily Eagle* on "Black Thursday" (October 24, 1929) announces the panic on Wall Street on the first day of the Stock Market Crash that would usher in the Great Depression.

banks were desperate to sell. Over 16 million shares were sold that day, and thousands of investors lost everything. Companies were left in ruins, and the banks lost the trust of the American people.

Although the 1929 crash was not the only cause of the Great Depression that followed, it is considered to be the beginning of the worst, most prolonged economic disaster in United States history. With the economy in shambles and the American Dream turned into a nightmare, the Jazz Age—what Fitzgerald later called "the most expensive orgy in history"—officially came to an end.

TWO

The Life of
F. Scott Fitzgerald

Francis Scott Key Fitzgerald was born on September 24, 1896, in St. Paul, Minnesota. His name—a nod to his ancestor Francis Scott Key, author of "The Star-Spangled Banner"—roots him to American culture, and Scott Fitzgerald (as he preferred to be called) would go on to write some of the most quintessentially American novels of his generation.

Family Background and Childhood

Scott Fitzgerald was the third child born to Edward Fitzgerald and Mary (Mollie) McQuillan Fitzgerald. The couple's first two daughters, aged one and three, died from an illness in 1896. After Scott was born, they had another daughter who died at birth in 1900. Scott's only living sibling, Annabel, was born in 1901.

Descended from Maryland families tracing back to the seventeenth century, Edward's family considered themselves Southern—as a child, Edward aided Confederate soldiers during the Civil War. Mollie McQuillan, on the other hand, was the daughter of Irish immigrant parents. Her father,

Phillip McQuillan, was the embodiment of the American Dream that is such a common theme in his grandson's work: he built his own business from the ground up, amassing a fortune that he left to Mollie and her siblings when he died.

Mollie's family money was both a great help and a source of tension for the Fitzgerald family. Edward's furniture company in St. Paul failed in 1898, and the family was forced to move around a lot—from St. Paul to Buffalo, to Syracuse, back to Buffalo, then back to St. Paul. It was Mollie's money and family connections that kept the family afloat during Fitzgerald's rootless childhood. Fitzgerald, however, was very class conscious. Though his mother's "new money" provided him with the best education available, he viewed himself as being from a lower social class than the children he associated with. He was conscious of his father's financial failures, yet he respected him and associated him with the old-stock American breeding that society valued over the new immigrant class.

Early Education

The Fitzgeralds were practicing Catholics, and Scott attended **parochial** school in Buffalo, where he began a practice of detailed record-keeping—notebooks, ledgers, clippings, correspondence—that would continue throughout his life. Nine-year-old Scott also believed that he was not his parents' child but royalty left on their doorstep, which was most likely a response to growing awareness and embarrassment regarding his father's failings. Insecurity regarding one's social position, combined with the belief one possessed superior intelligence, would become a recurring theme in his life and work.

Edward Fitzgerald lost his job in Buffalo in March 1908, and that summer the family returned to St. Paul. Scott attended St. Paul Academy, a private boys' school, where his passion for writing, sports, and social status grew. While he played football and baseball at St. Paul, he was never an exceptional athlete.

A portrait of the author at age 15, taken in 1911 when Fitzgerald was a student at the Newman School, a Catholic preparatory school in Hackensack, New Jersey.

Father Fay

Father Cyril Sigourney Webster Fay was a Catholic priest and trustee of the Newman School when Fitzgerald met him in November 1912. Fay was a wealthy, sophisticated, and well-traveled man who encouraged the young Fitzgerald to pursue his literary ambitions and reinforced his belief that he was destined for greatness.

Through Father Fay, Fitzgerald met Shane Leslie, a relative of Winston Churchill who had traveled the world, meeting famous literary figures such as Leo Tolstoy and William Butler Yeats. Fay and Leslie represented a more glamorous and romanticized version of the Catholic Church, and for a brief period Fitzgerald considered becoming a priest. However, Fitzgerald was never really committed to Catholicism and abandoned it completely later in life (though he would explore it in some of his work). Still, the importance of Father Fay to the young Fitzgerald is evident in the fact that the character of Monsignor Darcy in Fitzgerald's first novel, *This Side of Paradise* (1920), is closely based on Fay, and the novel itself is dedicated to him.

He was able to achieve some success with his writing at St. Paul, however. His first published story, "The Mystery of the Raymond Mortgage," appeared in the October 1909 issue of the school newspaper. In 1911, Fitzgerald wrote a play called *The Girl from Lazy J*, which was the earliest exploration of a common motif in his work: the young man willing to do anything to win the heart of a beautiful, desirable girl.

Fitzgerald showed much literary promise, but he was a poor student. His parents enrolled him in the Newman School, a prestigious Catholic preparatory school in New Jersey, for the remainder of high school. They hoped it would provide more academic discipline yet still surround him with peers of wealth and status. His second year at Newman brought him more social and literary success, with a number of his stories appearing in the *Newman News*. It was during his second year that Fitzgerald met and befriended Father Fay, who encouraged his literary ambitions and became a surrogate father to him.

Princeton University

Fitzgerald wrote that Princeton was "the pleasantest country club in America," and his interest in attending the university was based more on its social status and athletic program than on its academic reputation. He immediately tried out for the freshman football team in the fall of 1913, but his small stature and mediocre performance made his dream of becoming a campus football star impossible. The social scene at Princeton was even more cutthroat than it had been at his previous schools, and Fitzgerald, feeling again like an outcast, threw himself into his writing.

While his grades were still poor during his freshman year, Fitzgerald had some success writing for the school's humor magazine, and wrote a musical comedy for the Princeton Triangle Club. During this time he also formed two important, lifelong friendships: Edmund Wilson, who would go on to

Princeton University's Blair Hall is a stunning example of the Gothic-style architecture popular on college campuses in the late nineteenth and early twentieth centuries.

become an influential literary critic and editor, and John Peale Bishop, who was to become a successful novelist and poet, as well as the basis for the character Thomas Parke D'Invilliers in *This Side of Paradise*. Returning home to St. Paul for the Christmas holidays, Fitzgerald met his first love, Ginevra King.

A sixteen-year-old socialite from Lake Forest, Illinois, Ginevra King was everything Fitzgerald found attractive in a woman: beautiful, popular, and wealthy. The fact that she was sought after by other Ivy League suitors also made Ginevra that much more appealing to him. The two met at a party in King's honor at a St. Paul country club in January 1915, and Fitzgerald used their first encounter as the basis for the first meeting of **protagonist** Amory Blaine and his first love, Isabelle Borgé, in his novel *This Side of Paradise*.

Ginevra King inspired some of Fitzgerald's female characters, most notably Isabelle Borgé and Daisy Buchanan.

While Fitzgerald's social standing improved during his college years, his academic performance continued to be poor, and he was forced to leave Princeton during his junior year because of it (though he would always maintain it was due to illness). He considered this period one of the most devastating of his youth.

In the fall of 1916, Fitzgerald went back and repeated his junior year, but his grades did not improve. With his relationship with Ginevra King deteriorating and his campus social status in decline, he focused on his writing.

When America entered World War I on April 6, 1917, he enrolled in campus military training and took the infantry exam. On October 26, 1917, Fitzgerald was commissioned as a second lieutenant, ending his Princeton career. The fact that he never graduated remained one of the great disappointments of his life.

World War I and *The Romantic Egotist*

Fitzgerald reported for his army training in November 1917 at Fort Leavenworth, Kansas, convinced like so many other men of his generation that he would die overseas. During this time he completed a first draft of a novel called *The Romantic Egotist*. He sent it to Shane Leslie, who forwarded it to his

Scribner's editor Maxwell Perkins, who launched Fitzgerald's career as a professional author, is photographed at his desk in 1943.

own publisher, Charles Scribner's Sons. It was rejected, but not before it reached the desk of an editor named Maxwell Perkins. Perkins was the only editor at Scribner's who saw any promise in Fitzgerald's work, and he urged him in his rejection letter to revise and resubmit the manuscript with a more polished conclusion.

The armistice was announced on November 11, 1918, ending the war, and Fitzgerald never had the chance to serve overseas. Along with not graduating from Princeton, he considered not seeing battle to be one of his life's great failures. His military training was not completely in vain, however. While stationed at Camp Sheridan in Montgomery, Alabama, in the summer of 1918, Fitzgerald met eighteen-year-old Zelda Sayre, who would become central to his life and his work.

Zelda Sayre

Zelda Sayre was born on July 24, 1900 in Montgomery, Alabama. Her father, Alabama Supreme Court Judge Anthony Dickinson Sayre, and her mother, Minerva "Minnie" Machen Sayre, the daughter of a Kentucky senator, both came from

Zelda Sayre Fitzgerald, wearing ballet clothes and pointe shoes, poses for a photograph with her cat in 1928.

distinguished Southern families. Zelda, the youngest of five, was from a young age a free spirit. Popular, fun-loving, and rebellious, she took ballet as a young girl and had the grace and poise of a dancer. Scott fell madly in love with her.

Zelda embodied two separate cultures: the Old South and the "New Woman." Ambitious and independent, she wanted a glamorous, exciting life, but also desired the stability of traditional values. Though she loved Fitzgerald, she would not commit to him until he was financially secure and successful. His relationship with Zelda provided him with the motivation he needed to revise *The Romantic Egotist*, but it was rejected again. When Fitzgerald received his discharge he moved to New York City to look for work, knowing that he had to establish himself in order to win Zelda's hand in marriage.

Early Career and Marriage

Fitzgerald moved to New York only a few weeks after receiving the devastating news that his mentor, Monsignor Fay, had died. He took an unfulfilling job writing advertising slogans to support himself while he submitted short stories to magazines. His first bit of success came when his first professionally published story, "Babes in the Woods," appeared in *The Smart Set* in June 1919.

Despite this news, Zelda broke up with him in June, and Fitzgerald went on a drinking binge that ended on July 1, 1919 when the Wartime Prohibition Act went into effect. He later wrote about it in his essay, "My Lost City" (1936):

> I wandered through the town of 127th Street, resenting its vibrant life … I was a failure—mediocre at advertising work and unable to get started as a writer. Hating the city, I got roaring, weeping drunk on my last penny and went home.

Newlyweds Scott and Zelda Fitzgerald are photographed in their winter coats in early 1921.

Fitzgerald quit his job in early July and returned to St. Paul to focus on his novel, convinced that achieving literary fame was the only way to win Zelda back. He revised his earlier manuscript and changed the title from *The Romantic Egotist* to *The Education of a Personage* before finally settling on *This Side of Paradise*.

In early September, Fitzgerald sent the manuscript to Max Perkins. This time, Perkins was insistent; he wanted Scribner's to publish new, young talent like Fitzgerald and threatened to resign if they would not accept it. With his novel accepted and set for a spring 1920 release, a reinvigorated Fitzgerald spent the fall and winter on short stories, which he hoped would bring fast money.

The May 1, 1920 issue of *The Saturday Evening Post*, which published much of Fitzgerald's short fiction, was the first to feature Fitzgerald's name on the cover as a contributor for the story "Bernice Bobs Her Hair."

He signed with the Paul Revere Reynolds literary agency, where his agent, Harold Ober, got Fitzgerald's stories into *The Saturday Evening Post*, one of the most popular and widely circulated magazines of the time. "Head and Shoulders" (February 1920) was Fitzgerald's first story published in the Post, and "Bernice Bobs Her Hair" (May 1920)—

a flapper story based on a letter Fitzgerald wrote to his sister, Annabel, instructing her on how to achieve social success— was the first appearance of his name on the magazine's cover. Throughout his career, the majority of his income would come from short story sales. Fitzgerald would always be frustrated by the necessity of writing them for the income they supplied, because they interrupted progress on his novels.

With his literary success assured, Zelda finally agreed to marriage. *This Side of Paradise* was published on March 26, 1920, and Scott and Zelda were married on April 4 at St. Patrick's Cathedral in New York City. Fitzgerald had achieved his dreams at the young age of twenty-three, and he would later write that "the compensation of a very early success is a conviction that life is a romantic matter."

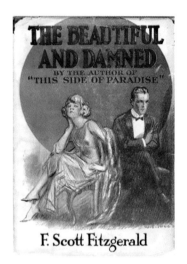

F. Scott Fitzgerald

The 1922 first edition of Fitzgerald's *The Beautiful and Damned* was illustrated by W.E. Hill and featured main characters Anthony and Gloria.

Success and Celebrity

Scott and Zelda's wedding coincided with the beginning of the Roaring Twenties, and the new couple epitomized the decade—they were young, beautiful, seemingly rich, and wild. However, in New York during the early months of their marriage, Scott was clearly in the early stages of alcoholism, and often embarrassed himself with his drunken behavior. Still, people were drawn to the Fitzgeralds for their charm and imagination.

Their relationship began to deteriorate early, with Zelda growing increasingly resentful of Scott's fame. She grew restless while he was writing, and would seek the company of other men. The couple began a pattern of fighting and making up that would characterize their marriage.

Fitzgerald submitted his second novel, *The Beautiful and Damned*, to Harold Ober for publication while he and Zelda were in St. Paul awaiting the birth of their daughter. Frances Scott "Scottie" Fitzgerald was born on October 26, 1921, and Zelda said that she wanted her daughter to be "a beautiful little fool." Fitzgerald later used the line in *The Great Gatsby* as Daisy's reaction to the birth of her daughter, Pammy.

Fitzgerald and Hemingway

In the spring of 1925, Scott met a young writer named Ernest Hemingway in Paris. Many years later, Hemingway would recount their first meeting in his memoir, *A Moveable Feast* (1964), where he describes Fitzgerald as a drunken fool, sexually inexperienced, and effeminate. The two would form a friendship, but Hemingway always remained judgmental about Fitzgerald. For his part, Fitzgerald was impressed with Hemingway's talent, as well as his service in the war and his athleticism—two things that Fitzgerald admired but had never achieved.

Personal feelings aside, Hemingway greatly respected *The Great Gatsby*, and introduced Fitzgerald to Gertrude Stein and the expatriate artist community in Paris. Fitzgerald, who took a great interest in Hemingway's work, successfully recruited him to Scribner's. Their friendship grew more strained over the years, and finally reached its breaking point when Hemingway publically shamed Fitzgerald in his story, "The Snows of Kilimanjaro" (1936), referring to him as "poor Scott Fitzgerald" and portraying him as a pitiful man who idolizes the rich. Though Fitzgerald continued to care for Hemingway and respect his work, the two would never be close again.

Seaside resort area Antibes, on the French Riviera, contains the town of Juan-les-Pins, where Scott and Zelda lived during part of their time in France in the mid-1920s.

After a successful serialization in *Metropolitan* magazine, a revised version of *The Beautiful and Damned* was published in March 1922. The novel is the story of a young couple, Anthony and Gloria Patch, who deteriorate as a result of alcohol and wasteful spending, which destroys Anthony's health and Gloria's beauty. Although not as well received as *This Side of Paradise*, it demonstrates an effort by Fitzgerald to present a more consistent narrative.

Long Island, Europe, and *The Great Gatsby*

The Fitzgeralds rented a home in Great Neck, Long Island in September of 1922, and it was here that Fitzgerald drew much of the material for the characters and setting of the novel that would become *The Great Gatsby*. After completing a number of short stories and articles on Jazz Age culture, the Fitzgerald family moved to Europe, where they felt they could live on less money.

The Fitzgeralds moved to the French Riviera in April 1924, where Scott wrote and revised the first draft of *Gatsby*. During this time, Zelda had a relationship with French aviator

The Fitzgeralds take a family portrait with their young daughter, Frances Scott "Scottie" Fitzgerald, in their Paris apartment in the mid-1920s.

Edouard Jozan. Fitzgerald was traumatized by the experience and lost faith in Zelda's love for him. This disillusionment was a major contributor to his characterization of Gatsby's relationship with Daisy. *The Great Gatsby* was published in April 1925, while the Fitzgeralds were living in Paris.

The Fitzgeralds remained in France, alternating between Paris and the Riviera, until late 1926. They continued to spend recklessly, and Fitzgerald's alcoholism escalated. Zelda began to exhibit mentally unstable behavior, and the two often fought in public. They returned to New York in December 1926, their finances and their marriage in complete disarray.

Zelda's First Breakdown

In early 1927, Fitzgerald was offered a writing job in Hollywood, where he met the young actress Lois Moran. Though there was no physical relationship, Zelda was bitterly jealous. Although Fitzgerald's script was rejected, he did gain material for his last two novels. Moran became the basis for the character of Rosemary Hoyt in *Tender Is the Night*, and director Irving Thalberg became the inspiration for Monroe Stahl, the main character in Fitzgerald's last and unfinished novel, *The Last Tycoon*.

In March 1927, the Fitzgeralds rented a mansion called Ellerslie near Wilmington, Delaware. Over the next two years, Zelda pursued creative outlets, partially in response to her jealousy of Moran and partially to carve out her own identity separate from her famous husband. Now in her late twenties, Zelda pursued the unrealistic goal of becoming a ballerina. She took up painting and wrote articles—though she resented the fact that magazines would only publish her work with Scott's name attached.

In April 1928 they returned to Paris, where he intended to finish his fourth novel and Zelda began training with the famous ballerina Lubov Egorova. When they left Paris in October, the novel was still incomplete, and Fitzgerald's drinking was getting out of hand again. Zelda's ballet had become an obsession, and she would practice for hours on end, often missing meals.

The Fitzgeralds returned to Europe in the spring of 1929. Zelda resumed her training with Egorova, while Fitzgerald continued to struggle with his novel.

Zelda began displaying mental problems. In October, she grabbed the wheel while Scott was driving and tried to run them off a cliff. At one point, she thought that the flowers in a market were speaking to her. She suffered her first major breakdown, and entered the Malmaison Clinic near Paris on April 23, 1930.

This rare UK edition of *Tender Is the Night* features artist Edward Pagram's dust jacket illustration of a cityscape that spans from the front to back cover.

Deterioration and *Tender Is the Night*

Zelda left Malmaison in May, but began experiencing hallucinations that resulted in attempted suicide. She entered a clinic in Switzerland less than two weeks later, and was diagnosed as **schizophrenic**. Her doctor thought it imperative that Zelda quit ballet in order to recover. Scott agreed, and asked Egorova to write to Zelda and convince her to give up.

Egorova's letter, while more positive than expected, made it clear that Zelda was too old to be a professional. Zelda took it hard and abandoned her dream, though she would continue to dance for pleasure.

Fitzgerald returned to America when his father died in January 1931, and Zelda made progress while he was gone. Upon her release in September, the Fitzgeralds returned to Montgomery. Scott received an offer to rewrite a screenplay, and while he was in Hollywood, Zelda's father died. Judge Sayre, though strict, had always been a source of stability in her life, and she suffered another breakdown. In February 1932, she was admitted to the Phipps Clinic in Baltimore.

While at Phipps, Zelda completed her largely auto-biographical novel, *Save Me the Waltz*. Fitzgerald was angry that she had sent it to Perkins without letting him read it. He felt that he had ownership of the material about their life together, which she had used while his own novel languished so he could pay for her care. Zelda revised the novel to his satisfaction, and it was published in October 1932. It was not successful.

Though Zelda was eventually released, there was no longer any hope of a full rehabilitation. Now living in Baltimore, the Fitzgeralds were faced with financial trouble—Scott's material was no longer right for the market, and the magazines, complaining about the decreased quality of his work, dropped the price paid for his stories. Despite his alcoholism and the continuing deterioration of his marriage, which almost resulted in divorce, Fitzgerald delivered the manuscript for *Tender Is the Night* to Scribner's in late October 1933.

Tender Is the Night was serialized in *Scribner's Magazine*, and the revised novel was published on April 12, 1934—nine years after the publication of *The Great Gatsby*. Drawing heavily on Zelda's mental breakdown and Fitzgerald's own failings, it is the story of the decline of Dick Diver, a once-brilliant

The Fitzgeralds attend a formal event in 1935, during the "Crack-Up" period when Zelda was frequently institutionalized and Scott was suffering the effects of severe alcoholism.

psychiatrist who marries his wealthy patient, Nicole Warren. The novel reflects Fitzgerald's own personal and professional deterioration in the years after the publication of Gatsby, and revisits his common theme of the corrupting influence of wealth.

The Crack-Up

Zelda suffered a third breakdown in February 1934, and attempted suicide multiple times while institutionalized in 1935. Fitzgerald's own health was rapidly deteriorating, and he moved to North Carolina to seek treatment for tuberculosis and alcoholism. In November, he wrote "The Crack-Up," the first in a series of confessional essays published in *Esquire* magazine that explore his deterioration and professional failures.

In "The Crack-Up," Fitzgerald writes, "I began to realize that for two years my life had been a drawing on resources that I did not possess, that I had been mortgaging myself physically and spiritually up to the hilt." In this essay, and those that followed it, Fitzgerald associates his failings with an emotional bankruptcy and loss of vitality. The essays, while excellent, were not received well at the time and harmed his reputation as a professional writer. His career appeared to be finished, and people found his exhibitionist self-pity disgraceful. To an America suffering through the Depression years, Fitzgerald represented all the excesses of the Jazz Age and the inevitable decline that came with them.

Things only got worse for Fitzgerald in 1936: Zelda was suffering from a religious mania, he was publicly humiliated in Hemingway's story "The Snows of Kilimanjaro," and his mother died. The crushing blow came from *New York Post* journalist Michael Mok, whose scathing article in September 1936 described Fitzgerald as a washed up, depressed alcoholic who had lost all hope for his future. After reading the article, Fitzgerald overdosed on morphine, but it caused him to vomit and did no permanent damage.

Hollywood and The Last Tycoon

In late June 1937, film studio Metro-Goldwyn-Mayer offered Fitzgerald a job. Desperate for money, he accepted and moved back to Hollywood in July 1937, where he met a twenty-eight-year-old gossip columnist named Sheilah Graham. They quickly developed a relationship that lasted until the end of his life.

Fitzgerald did not thrive in the team writing approach popular at the time, and when MGM did not renew Fitzgerald's contract, he was forced to search for freelance work in Hollywood to make ends meet. His alcoholism continued to be a problem. In April 1939, during a trip with Zelda to Havana, Cuba, he left her alone in a hotel room while he went out drinking. He was beaten by spectators at a cockfight, leaving Zelda responsible for getting him to New York and checking him into a hospital. It was the last time Scott and Zelda would ever be together.

Between late 1939 and into 1940, Fitzgerald made significant progress on his fifth and final novel, though he

Gossip columnist Sheilah Graham, pictured here in 1945, maintained a romantic relationship with Fitzgerald from 1927 until his death in 1940.

would not finish it. Published posthumously by his Princeton classmate Edmund Wilson as *The Last Tycoon* (changed to *The Love of the Last Tycoon: A Western* in a later edition), it is the story of Monroe Stahl, a visionary Hollywood producer (based on Irving Thalberg), and his conflict with rival producer, Pat Brady. Though the novel was never completed, the working drafts and notes for the novel suggest it would have rivaled *Gatsby* in its examination of the American Dream.

Death and Revival

In November 1940, Fitzgerald suffered a cardiac episode in a drugstore and moved in with Sheilah. His health seemed to be improving under her care, but on December 21, 1940, F. Scott Fitzgerald died of a heart attack while making notes on the

The gravestone of F. Scott and Zelda Fitzgerald, located in St. Mary's Catholic Cemetery in Rockville, Maryland.

football team in *The Princeton Alumni* magazine.

As a non-practicing Catholic, Fitzgerald was buried in Rockville Union Cemetery in Rockville, Maryland, on December 27. (Scottie would later have both of her parents moved to the Fitzgerald family plot in St. Mary's Catholic Cemetery.) Despite being one of America's most famous literary figures, Fitzgerald's entire estate only amounted to $35,000. There were still unsold copies of his books in the warehouse at the time of his death.

The Fitzgerald literary revival started almost immediately after his death. Edmund Wilson edited and published the unfinished manuscript of *The Last Tycoon* in 1941, with *The Great Gatsby* and five short stories included in the volume. An armed services edition of *The Great Gatsby* was available during World War II, and a number of collections of his short stories and novels were published. Almost everything that Fitzgerald ever wrote—including his thoughtbook, his notebooks, his ledgers, and the extensive correspondence he kept—has been published and studied. There are periodicals devoted solely to his work, and museums and libraries dedicated to him. Though he died before he was able to revive his career, thinking he would be forgotten, F. Scott Fitzgerald lives on in his work as the most important writer of Jazz Age America.

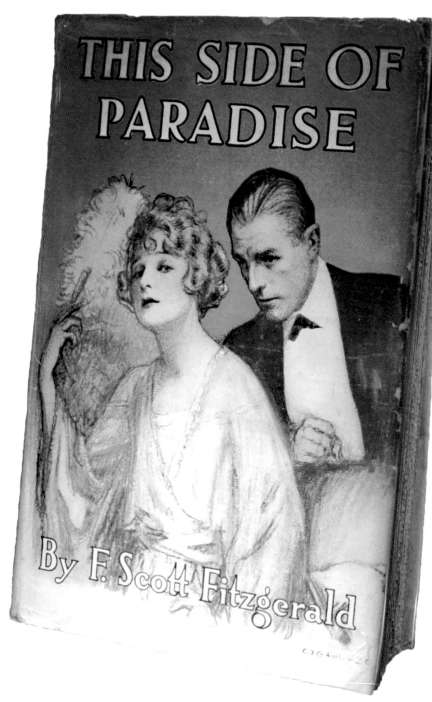

This 1920 first edition of *This Side of Paradise* includes
the original dust jacket illustrated by W. E. Hill.

THREE

This Side of Paradise

This Side of Paradise was published on March 26, 1920, and the first printing sold out in just three days. Generally well received by critics, it was universally popular among American youth, solidifying Fitzgerald as the spokesman and chronicler of a generation at a time of major social and cultural change in America.

Plot Summary

This Side of Paradise is the story of Amory Blaine, whose **idealism** leads him to believe he is destined for great things. The novel is divided into two books—"The Romantic Egotist" and "The Education of a Personage"—separated by an interlude in the form of two letters written during Amory's wartime service.

Book One begins with Amory as a young boy traveling around the county with his wealthy, eccentric mother, Beatrice. When Beatrice suffers a nervous breakdown, Amory is forced to stay in Minneapolis with relatives. His mother's influence has left Amory with an inflated sense of self that makes him an outsider among his peers. At age thirteen, Amory courts Myra St. Claire and has his first kiss, after which "sudden revulsion seized [him], disgust, loathing for the whole incident." This is the first of many instances where Amory demonstrates a puritanical attitude toward sexuality that is uncharacteristic of his generation.

Before Amory leaves the Midwest to attend St. Regis Prep School in Connecticut, he meets a Catholic priest, Monsignor Thayer Darcy, an old friend of his mother's, who becomes a mentor and father figure to him. Despite a difficult first year, he later graduates as the star quarterback and the editor of the school paper.

Amory enters his freshman year at Princeton with the desire to be "one of the gods of the class." Failing at football and lazy when it comes to academics, he focuses on literary pursuits. He makes friends—brothers Kerry and Burne Holiday, Thomas Parke D'Invilliers, and Dick Humbird—who, in different ways, will influence the way he views himself and the world.

Princeton's Alexander Hall, designed by William A. Potter and dedicated in 1894, was the last of the High Victorian Gothic buildings erected on the university's campus.

During Christmas break of his sophomore year, he meets his first love, Isabelle Borgé. Soon after, he is elected into the exclusive Cottage Club—a sign for Amory that he "had arrived."

Amory, returning from a party in New York with his friends, discovers that Dick Humbird has crashed his car and died—an incident that will haunt Amory for the rest of his life. He is briefly distracted from his grief by a visit to the Borgés' Long Island home, during which he kisses Isabelle. As with Myra St. Claire, Amory becomes disillusioned and realizes that "he had not an ounce of real affection" for Isabelle. The two soon break up, and Amory begins a downward spiral.

Amory fails a make-up examination and becomes ineligible for the leadership positions he thought he was destined for. After losing all he had gained at Princeton, Amory learns that his father has died and his family's fortune is in decline. In despair, he visits Monsignor Darcy, feeling he has "lost half [his] personality in a year." Monsignor Darcy disagrees, and urges Amory to start fresh so that he can move toward "the next thing." Amory returns to Princeton.

Disillusioned with his professors and envious of Kerry Holiday's decision to join the war, Amory visits New York with a friend, Fred Sloane. While they are out on the town with two showgirls, Amory notices a strange man watching him. He sees the figure again later in showgirl Axia Marlowe's apartment. Amory finally comes face-to-face with the grotesque devil figure in an alley. To his horror, he sees Dick Humbird's face flash before him.

The title of the final chapter of Book One, "Narcissus Off Duty," is significant in its reference to the Greek myth of Narcissus, whose vanity causes him to fall in love with his own reflection in a pool of water and drown. Amory, whose own vanity and egotism has brought him down, begins to look outside himself when his friend Burne Holiday leads an anti-club movement at Princeton. Admiring Burne's rejection

The clubhouse of the Princeton University Cottage Club, of which Fitzgerald and his fictional counterpart, Amory Blaine, were members, was constructed in 1906.

of conformity and rebellion against the school's social caste system, Amory realizes that "all his mental processes of the last year and a half seemed stale and futile—a petty consummation of himself." Through Burne, he is able to shed the self-absorption and obsession with status that has been holding him back from his great destiny.

Another positive influence on Amory at this time is Clara Page, his widowed cousin, with whom he falls in love. Clara has found freedom in her widowhood, is happy with her two children, and refuses to marry again. She represents for Amory all that is good and pure. Clara tells him that he is a slave to his imagination, and that his true weakness is his lack of good judgment. In breaking down Amory's egotism, she enables him to move forward to "the next thing," and Amory says goodbye to Princeton and joins the armed forces.

"Interlude: May, 1917–February, 1919" is comprised of two letters and a short poem, which divides the novel's two parts. In the first letter, from Monsignor Darcy to Amory, the priest expresses his horror at the war and at what he sees as Amory's inevitable spiritual death. In the poem, Amory predicts he will look back on the war years as futile. The section ends with a letter from Amory, stationed in Germany, to Tom D'Invilliers. He writes of the death of his mother and the further depletion of his family fortune.

Book Two, "The Education of a Personage," opens with a chapter written as a play, where Amory meets and falls in love with Rosalind Connage, his roommate Alec's sister. Rosalind is beautiful, self-absorbed, and thoroughly modern. They fall immediately and intensely in love with each other. She rejects a wealthy suitor, Dawson Ryder, whom her mother considers a more appropriate match.

Amory takes a job at an advertising agency in New York in order to make enough money to marry Rosalind, but ultimately she breaks up with him, telling Amory that she would not be the woman he loves if forced to struggle without money while he makes his start.

Amory, devastated by his breakup with Rosalind, quits his job and goes on a self-destructive drinking binge in New York until Prohibition turns the country dry. Emotionally drained and bored, he throws himself into literature and conversation with his roommate, Tom, claiming that the war "killed individualism out of our generation."

Tom's mother becomes ill and he moves home. Amory heads to Washington to visit Monsignor Darcy, but having just missed him he goes instead to Maryland to visit an uncle. Amory is forced to seek shelter during a violent storm and meets Eleanor Savage, a beautiful and reckless young woman. A self-described "romantic little materialist," she and Amory have an intense summer romance. When Eleanor nearly rides her horse off a cliff to prove she is an atheist, Amory realizes that as he "had loved himself in Eleanor, so now what he hated was only a mirror." She is the last of Amory's loves, and though the two keep in contact over the years and exchange poems, their passion is just a fond memory.

Amory goes to Atlantic City and runs into Alec Connage. They lament the death of college friends Jesse Ferrenby and Kerry Holiday in the war. Amory falls into a deep despair, mourning his lost youth and the loss of Rosalind.

Amory agrees to share a hotel room with Alec and falls asleep. He is awoken by Alec, who has taken up with a girl named Jill and is about to be discovered by the house detective. Amory takes the blame for Alec's sexual misconduct with an unmarried woman, but knows that his "supercilious sacrifice" (as the chapter is named) is "by its very nature … arrogant and impersonal." He does not do it for Alec; still the romantic egotist, he does it for himself. In the same paper that published his crime, he sees Rosalind and Dawson Ryder's engagement announcement. Soon after, he receives notice that his fortune had been lost to poor investments, and a telegram informing him of Monsignor Darcy's death. Amory is left with nothing; he has lost his money, his love, and the only person left in the world that he could rely on for support.

In New York, Amory realizes he has lost his faith, realizing that "there were no more wise men … no more heroes" and feels the urge to "let himself go to the devil" by escaping to an exotic place where he could indulge himself in vice and lust. Monsignor Darcy's funeral stirs something in him, however, and he has an epiphany: He no longer wants to be loved and admired, but to be indispensable to people and give them a sense of security, as Monsignor Darcy and Burne Holiday did for him.

He sets off on a walk to Princeton, and along the way he is picked up by the father of his dead college friend, Jesse Ferrenby, and they talk about socialism. When Amory reaches the school, he finds it populated by a "new generation dedicated more than the last to the fear of poverty and the worship of success; grown up to find all Gods dead, all wars fought, all faiths in man shaken" and he pities them. Despite his own lost faith and without knowing exactly why, Amory decides to continue his struggle toward a great destiny. The novel ends with the egotist becoming a personage, as Amory exclaims to the sky: "I know myself, but that is all."

Cultural Context

World War I divides *This Side of Paradise* as it divided the nation, with the postwar generation coming of age during a period of cultural upheaval and finding themselves in conflict with the traditional values of their elders. The novel captures Jazz Age culture: the sexually liberated "New Woman;" the focus on materialism, wealth, and success; the loss of faith; and the socialist countercultural movement all feature prominently.

The first ads for the book featured Fitzgerald's slogan— "a novel about flappers written for philosophers." The novel was the first to realistically depict flapper culture, and Fitzgerald writes frankly about petting parties, which was quite shocking at the time.

A typical flapper girl, with her bobbed hair, cloche hat, short hemline, and stockinged legs, lounges and smokes a cigarette, circa 1925.

In Rosalind, one sees the Jazz Age focus on material wealth and success. Despite her love for Amory and her unconventional ways, she ultimately marries Dawson Ryder for the money and stability he provides. Wealth is also important to Amory. The desire for success lies at the heart of his romantic egotism and the conviction that some great destiny awaits him. Like so many people during the Roaring Twenties, Amory is convinced that the American Dream of wealth, fame, and success is there for the taking.

Though from humble beginnings, oil tycoon John D. Rockefeller became one of the world's wealthiest men.

While the Jazz Age was mostly characterized by consumption and the mindless pursuit of wealth, there was an active radical faction in America at the time. Burne Holiday's rejection of Princeton's elitist caste system and Amory's later arguments against capitalism represent this "other" America. By the end of the novel, Amory begins to consider socialist principles, having realized that the pursuit of success and wealth is shallow and will not bring him any closer to self-realization. Published at the very beginning of the decade that would see untold prosperity in America, Fitzgerald accurately predicts that the pursuit of wealth and success would do more harm than good.

The loss of faith and the sense of disillusionment that swept the country after the war's end are captured vividly in Amory's downfall in Book Two. Returning soldiers had experienced meaningless death and destruction in the name of democracy. Like Amory, they came home to discover their values and beliefs were replaced by the new culture of the American celebrity, and that the worship of the dollar was the new national religion.

Major Characters

Amory Blaine

Fitzgerald's alter ego, Amory is ambitious and believes he is destined for great things, but the same egotism that drives him consistently gets in his way. His romantic egotism dooms him to repeat the same pattern: he is propelled towards his destiny, falls in love with a woman who disappoints him, loses himself in despair, then recovers his fundamental self and moves again toward some unknown future.

Monsignor Thayer Darcy

Monsignor Darcy is Amory's mentor and spiritual father. Literary, well-traveled, and wealthy, he represents the romantic, glamorous side of the Catholic Church. Though he tries to get Amory more involved in Catholicism, Amory's interest in the Church does not extend much farther than Darcy himself. Fitzgerald's own childhood mentor, Father Sigourney Fay, is the basis for the character of Darcy.

Isabelle Borgé

Isabelle, a Baltimore debutante, is Amory's first love. She has modeled her personality on popular novels, and because of this she is very artificial. Amory recognizes this and acknowledges that he has some of the same qualities. Their affair is innocent, ending not long after their first kiss when they get into an argument and Isabelle chastises Amory for his egotism. He realizes he never really had feelings for her, and only wanted to prove he could win her. Isabelle is based on Fitzgerald's own first love, Ginevra King.

Rosalind Connage

Rosalind, Alec Connage's sister, is the great love of Amory's life. A beautiful New York debutante, she initially rebels against convention by smoking, drinking, and having relationships with various men. Rosalind ultimately chooses stability over love. She breaks up with Amory, whom she does not believe will be able to provide her with the life of wealth and leisure she desires, and agrees to marry Dawson Ryder. Rosalind is partially based on Zelda Fitzgerald.

Burne Holiday

Of all Amory's college friends, Burne has the greatest influence on him. Burne leads an anti-club reform movement on campus that inspires Amory to look outside of himself and rethink the qualities he values in others. He respects Burne for his intellect, as opposed to the more superficial qualities he once admired in people like Dick Humbird. Burne becomes a socialist and a pacifist during the war, and while Amory does not entirely share in Burne's beliefs, he greatly respects them and admires Burne for going against the status quo. Burne is based on Fitzgerald's classmate at Princeton, Henry Strater, who led the anti-club movement during his junior year.

Dick Humbird

Good-looking and popular, Dick is a college friend of Amory's. Although he comes from "new money," Amory considers him aristocratic and honorable—the epitome of what the upper class should be. Dick dies in an automobile accident on the way back from a party in New York, and his death is Amory's first experience with mortality. Amory is later haunted by Dick's face during a night of drunken revelry in New York.

Clara Page

Amory's widowed cousin Clara is the only woman who does not return his love. Content just to care for her two children and never marry again, she represents the virtuous woman of the past. She is the only woman that is able to correctly analyze him and tell him exactly what is wrong with his egotistical approach to life. Clara is based on Fitzgerald's cousin, Cecilia Taylor.

Eleanor Savage

Eleanor is a beautiful, modern young woman with whom Amory has a relationship over a summer spent in Maryland. More so than any other female character, Eleanor represents the flapper: with a slim build and bobbed hair, she is wild and impetuous, criticizes the restrictions of her gender, and flaunts convention at every turn. Their romance fails when Eleanor nearly rides off a cliff to prove her atheism to Amory, and he sees that she is far too reckless and dangerous to be around.

Major Themes

Vocation

One of the main themes of the novel is the search for a vocation—a calling that gives life purpose and meaning. Amory believes he has a great destiny, but he does not know what it is. He searches for it in various places: social status, wealth, religion, and love, but all of these things ultimately disappoint and disillusion him. By the end of the novel, Amory realizes that what he wants is not to be admired or loved but to be "necessary to people, to be indispensible … to give people a sense of security." At the close of the novel, he begins to look outside of himself, and the conventions of American society, for purpose and meaning.

Despite the shift in social mores taking place in the 1920s, a woman's vocation was to find a husband to support her. This is most clearly demonstrated by Isabelle, who happily plays at courtship, "a game that would presumably be her principal study for years to come." Rosalind initially rejects this vocation, but ultimately accepts her fate and marries Dawson Ryder. Of all the women, Eleanor most strongly objects to the role society has defined for her, finding herself "with the brains to do everything, yet tied to the sinking ship of matrimony." While the novel does not explore Eleanor's fate, the poems she and Amory exchange years later give the impression that her youthful rebellion was fleeting.

A chauffer opens the door of a luxurious Rolls Royce limousine for his passenger.

Materialism

Fitzgerald's main drive to write *This Side of Paradise* came from his love for Zelda, who would not marry him unless he could provide for her. It is no surprise, then, that a major theme in the novel is materialism. From a very young age, Amory is obsessed with wealth and status. He values things that are superficial: good looks, athletic ability, popularity, and money. He is drawn to beautiful, materialistic women like Isabelle and Rosalind, who ultimately disappoint him—Isabelle because she has no real substance, and Rosalind because she is willing to give up the great love of her life for money.

As the novel progresses, Amory's family fortune dwindles down to nothing and he fails to become successful in New York. By the end of the book he is bankrupt, and begins to argue socialist ideals with the capitalist Mr. Ferrenby. While not entirely committed to becoming a Socialist like Burne Holiday, Amory is attracted to it because it stands in opposition to the capitalist America that has failed him. By the novel's end, Amory has abandoned his pursuit of personal gain and wants to dedicate his life to serving others. In his transition from an egotist to a personage, he sheds his materialism.

Major Symbol: The Supernatural

The supernatural element to *This Side of Paradise* corresponds with situations where Amory is confronted with sexuality. Amory's first kiss with Myra St. Claire repulses him, and when she asks him to kiss her again, Fitzgerald writes that "her voice came out of a great void." The most blatant supernatural example is Amory's hallucination of the devil/Dick Humbird's ghost at showgirl Axia Marlowe's apartment. Years later, in an Atlantic City hotel room, Amory perceives a strange aura around Alec Connage's date, Jill, lying in the bed, as well as a "dynamic shadow" among the curtains of the room. Amory's relationship with Eleanor Savage is filled with allusions to evil and the devil—she was "the last time evil crept close to Amory." At the end of the book, Fitzgerald explicitly states that, "the problem of evil had solidified for Amory into the problem of sex."

Increasingly liberal attitudes toward sex can be seen as symbolic of the decay of traditional values in postwar America. With the sexually liberated woman dominating film and magazines, the New Woman and the petting party became the norm. Fitzgerald himself (who was raised Catholic) was sexually conservative compared to some of his contemporaries, so it is possible that the equation of sex and death reflects what he personally saw as America's moral decline. Ironically, *This Side of Paradise* became almost required reading for college students at the time, and many young people used it as a guidebook for their collegiate experience.

This 1925 first edition printing of *The Great Gatsby*, with the famous dust jacket illustration by Francis Cugat, was displayed at the 2013 London International Antiquarian Book Fair.

FOUR

The Great Gatsby

Fitzgerald's third novel, *The Great Gatsby*, was published on April 10, 1925, and though it received excellent reviews and would become one of the most important and widely studied novels in American literature, sales were initially disappointing. There were still unsold copies of the book in the warehouse when Fitzgerald died in 1940.

After his first two novels, which were largely autobiographical and less structured, Fitzgerald wanted to write something that would display his technique and skill as a literary artist. He also felt it was important to showcase his talent as a novelist after focusing his energy on short stories, which he believed to be an artistically inferior endeavor.

Plot Summary

The Great Gatsby is both a story about one man's relentless pursuit of a dream and the American Dream itself. Jay Gatsby, born James Gatz, reinvents himself as a rich, successful man in order to win the love of his dream girl, Daisy Buchanan.

This mansion in Sands Point, New York, was owned by newspaper mogul William Randolph Hearst and is thought to be the inspiration for Gatsby's mansion.

Ultimately, Gatsby's idealized version of Daisy does not correspond to the reality of the woman, and he is destroyed when he realizes that his dream is hollow. Like Gatsby's Daisy, the American Dream of material wealth and success is completely meaningless and corrupts the life of anyone who pursues it. The story begins as it ends: with its narrator, Nick Carraway, reflecting back on the events that the novel chronicles,

which took place years earlier in the summer of 1922.

Nick Carraway is both a character and the sole narrator of the story. By presenting the main storyline as part of the past, Fitzgerald immediately gives Nick's judgments and assessments of the situation more weight. This lends a level of credibility to the narrative that was previously absent from Fitzgerald's work.

After a privileged childhood in a prominent Minnesota family, Nick attends Yale and serves overseas in World War I. After his discharge, he finds a job on Wall Street and rents a small bungalow in West Egg, Long Island—the less fashionable of the two identical formations of land separated by a bay. East Egg is home to those with old money and good breeding. West Egg is populated by the newly rich, who are considered inferior and looked down upon. Despite Nick's upbringing, he finds himself on West Egg in the shadow of Gatsby's mansion, and this sets up his position throughout the novel: Nick is both an actor and an observer, at the same time "within and without."

Nick travels to East Egg to visit his cousin, Daisy Buchanan, and her husband, Tom. Daisy and Tom are incredibly wealthy, and spent the years before drifting "here and there wherever people played polo and were rich together." Tom is a physically imposing man, and even his posture is arrogant and aggressive.

He takes Nick inside, where they find Daisy and her friend, Jordan Baker, lazy and motionless on the couch. Jordan, a professional golfer, appears haughty and bored. Nick finds himself attracted to her. When Jordan asks Nick if he is from West Egg and remarks that she knows Gatsby, Daisy suddenly becomes animated and asks, "What Gatsby?" Before Nick can answer, Tom announces dinner and moves Nick from the room "as though he were moving a checker to another square." From the beginning, Tom is shown using people like objects in a game.

Amateur golf champion Edith Cummings, who inspired the character of Jordan Baker, was the first female athlete featured on the cover of *Time* magazine.

Dinner is interrupted by a phone call for Tom. When Daisy follows her husband, Jordan tells Nick that Tom is having an affair with a woman in New York. The dinner ends awkwardly with the phone ringing again, and Daisy and Nick move to the front porch. During their conversation, Daisy tells Nick that, when the nurse told her that her baby was a girl, she cried and said, "I hope she'll be a fool—that's the best thing a girl can be in this world, a beautiful little fool." In that moment, Nick realizes that she is completely insincere, and he returns home to West Egg. Nick sees Gatsby for the first time that night, standing on his lawn with outstretched arms, staring off in the distance at a green light across the bay.

One afternoon, on their way to New York, Tom forces Nick off the train to meet his mistress in the valley of ashes, a poor, working-class area in the borough of Queens. The valley is an industrial dumping ground halfway between West Egg and New York, and overlooking it are the eyes of Doctor T. J. Eckleburg, remnants of an old billboard advertisement. The eyes "look out of no face but, instead, from a pair of enormous yellow spectacles" and "brood on over the solemn dumping

Broadway producer David Belasco is photographed in Atlantic City, New Jersey, on July 25, 1929.

ground." In contrast to glittering East Egg, the valley of ashes is a barren and desolate wasteland. On the edge of the valley is a garage owned by George Wilson, the husband of Tom's lover, Myrtle. Tom takes Nick into the garage and strings George along about the prospect of selling him his car. When Myrtle comes downstairs, Tom discreetly tells her to come to New York.

The three take the train to the city—with Myrtle riding in a separate car—and head uptown to the apartment that Tom keeps for her. Myrtle takes on an air of superiority as they reach her apartment. Much like Myrtle herself, the décor is pretentious and out of place. Myrtle invites her sister, Catherine, and her downstairs neighbors, the McKees, and they have a party where Nick gets drunk for the second time in his life.

Myrtle's sister mentions attending one of Gatsby's parties and shares the rumor that he is related to Kaiser Wilhelm, the ruler of Germany during WWI. This is the first of many speculations about Gatsby's past and where his money comes from. Everyone gets extremely drunk, and Nick is both repulsed and fascinated by the spectacle. The party ends when Myrtle repeatedly yells Daisy's name at Tom, who hits her and breaks her nose.

Soon after, Nick is personally invited to one of Gatsby's parties, differentiating him from most of the guests. Gatsby's parties were open to the public, like an amusement park, and people came for the spectacle. Among a sea of strangers, Nick encounters Jordan and attaches himself to her. Soon he hears more rumors about Gatsby from a pair of young flapper girls, one of whom claims he killed a man, but Nick does not believe it.

Jordan and Nick go in search of their host and find themselves in his library, where they encounter a drunken man who is amazed by the fact that the books on the shelves are real. The man, known only as Owl Eyes in the text, refers to Gatsby as "a regular Belasco"—a reference to Broadway producer David Belasco—implying that the library is no more than a theatrical set that Gatsby has taken great pains to craft realistically. The fact that the books' pages are not cut shows that Gatsby hasn't read them, providing further evidence of his artificiality.

Back at the party, Nick meets a man who turns out to be Gatsby. Nick is taken with his smile, which had a quality of "eternal reassurance" and "seemed to face … the whole external world for an instant, and then concentrated on you." When Gatsby's smile vanishes Nick sees him differently, noticing that the formal way in which he speaks borders on the absurd and that he seems to be choosing his words carefully. When Gatsby is called to the phone on unknown business, Nick asks Jordan about his background. She replies that she heard he was an Oxford man but does not believe it, though she cannot explain why. Jordan is later summoned to a private conversation with Gatsby. When she returns, she keeps their conversation a secret at Gatsby's request.

After leaving Gatsby's party, Nick interrupts the narrative to explain that there was much more to his summer than the parties he described. He comments on the everyday activities of his job and the excitement he felt in New York: "the racy, adventurous feel of it at night and the satisfaction that the constant flicker of men and women and machines give to the restless eye." He has started seeing Jordan romantically over the course of the summer, and although she is "incurably dishonest" as a result of her privileged upbringing, Nick finds himself attracted to her. This echoes his feelings about New York, which he finds both morally corrupt and exciting.

Returning to the narrative, Gatsby and Nick go to New York in Gatsby's flashy yellow car. On the way, Gatsby tells Nick an elaborate story about his past, claiming to be the son of wealthy midwestern parents (though he claims to be from San Francisco) who died and left him their fortune. He says he was educated at Oxford but seems to choke on the words, leaving Nick with a feeling that he is lying. He goes on to list other accomplishments, which seem rehearsed and laughable to Nick, ending with his acts as a war hero. Gatsby carries with him proof of his story—he produces a medal of valor from Montenegro and a photograph of himself at Oxford. As they cross over the Queensboro Bridge into New York, Nick starts to believe that "anything can happen … Even Gatsby could happen, without any particular wonder."

At lunch, Gatsby introduces Nick to Meyer Wolfshiem, who confuses Nick for a potential business associate. Gatsby later tells Nick that Wolfshiem is a gambler and the man responsible for fixing the 1919 World Series. When they run into Tom Buchanan, Nick introduces him to Gatsby, who appears uncomfortable and disappears when Nick turns his head.

That afternoon, Nick meets Jordan for tea at the Plaza Hotel and she tells him the details of her conversation with Gatsby: the story of when he and Daisy first met in October

1917. Daisy Fay was eighteen and the most celebrated belle in Louisville, Kentucky. Gatsby was a lieutenant stationed at nearby Camp Taylor, and one of Daisy's many suitors. The two fell in love, and although Daisy was devastated when Gatsby left for the war, she soon put him out of her mind and continued the privileged life of a debutante. She became engaged to Tom, who gave her a pearl necklace worth $350,000 as a wedding gift. The night before the wedding, Daisy received a letter from Gatsby and got drunk for the first time. She threw Tom's pearls in the trash and wanted to call off the wedding. However, half an hour later the pearls were back around her neck, and she married him the next day without incident.

When Jordan tells Nick that Gatsby bought his West Egg mansion to be across the bay from Daisy, Gatsby "came alive to [Nick], delivered suddenly from the womb of his purposeless splendor." Jordan finally asks Nick Gatsby's favor—that he invite Daisy to his bungalow and allow Gatsby to come over. Nick arranges the meeting as requested.

Their reunion at Nick's is awkward at first, and Gatsby believes he has made a terrible mistake. Nick leaves them alone for a while and when he returns, he finds Daisy's face wet with tears of joy and Gatsby glowing. The trio goes to Gatsby's mansion. With Daisy in his house for the first time, Gatsby revalues everything according to the response it draws from her. He looks at his things "as though in her actual and astounding presence none of it was any longer real." Gatsby has gone through a series of rapidly changing emotions since his reunion with Daisy: embarrassment, joy, and finally a sense of wonder at the fact that the dream that had consumed him for so long was finally within his grasp. When Gatsby mentions to Daisy that he can see the green light at the end of her dock from his house, it occurs to him that, with Daisy next to him, the light no longer holds significance and "his count of enchanted objects had diminished by one." Before he leaves the two alone,

Nick wonders if Daisy could ever possibly live up to Gatsby's expectations.

At this point, Gatsby is at the height of his notoriety, and Nick interrupts the main story to reveal part of the truth of Gatsby's past. Jay Gatsby was born James Gatz in North Dakota. His parents were unsuccessful farmers, and he spent his youth rejecting his true self and dreaming of a better life. At age seventeen, James Gatz encountered the wealthy Dan Cody aboard his yacht, and warned Cody that it was unsafe to drop anchor. Cody's yacht represented "all the beauty and glamour in the world," and as he approached it in his rowboat, James Gatz became Jay Gatsby. Cody, who had made his money as a prospector in the West, employed Gatsby on his yacht and traveled the world with him. Though Cody left Gatsby $25,000 when he died, Cody's mistress kept him from inheriting it. He was left only with the fully developed identity of Jay Gatsby and the drive to become wealthy and successful.

Not having seen Gatsby for weeks, Nick goes to his mansion, where a man named Mr. Sloane drops in on horseback with Tom and a woman. Gatsby is unnerved by Tom's presence but plays the gracious host, although he cannot resist mentioning to Tom that he knows Daisy. The woman facetiously invites Gatsby to dinner, but he cannot see that they do not really want him to come. The group leaves on horseback as Gatsby, who does not own a horse, prepares to take his car. The fact that Nick has already revealed Gatsby's past to the reader makes the event that much more awkward—even the identity Gatsby has created for himself is not good enough for the East Eggers.

This becomes even more apparent when Daisy finally attends one of Gatsby's parties. She arrives with Tom, and although the party is much the same as the others Nick has attended, their presence affects the way he sees things. Having grown accustomed to the parties, and West Egg itself, Nick now sees it all through Daisy's eyes and he finds it harsh and uncomfortable.

Gatsby tells Nick what he truly wants from Daisy: that she erase the past by telling Tom she never loved him. When Nick claims that you can't repeat the past, Gatsby is incredulous, crying out, "Can't repeat the past? Why of course you can!" Upset that Daisy did not like the party, Gatsby stops throwing them, and "as obscurely as it had begun, his career as Trimalchio was over." (Trimalchio is a character in an ancient Roman satire, Petronius's *Satyricon*, who hosts ostentatious parties.)

On the longest day of the year, Gatsby and Nick are invited to the Buchanan mansion, where Gatsby meets Daisy's daughter for the first time. He is taken aback by her presence—the child is tangible proof that the past five years existed, and it makes Gatsby uncomfortable. When Tom sees a look exchanged between Daisy and Gatsby, he realizes that she is in love with him and grows agitated, insisting the group go to New York. Tom drives Gatsby's car with Nick and Jordan, and Daisy and Gatsby take Tom's coupé. When they stop at George Wilson's garage for gas on the way, Wilson tells Tom that he and Myrtle are planning to go west. Nick sees Myrtle in the window, staring angrily at Jordan, whom she believes is Tom's wife.

k City's Plaza Hotel, which opened
, took two years to build and cost
lion, making it the most expensive
uilt in America at the time.

Realizing he is losing both his mistress and his wife, Tom drives to New York in a panic, where they all take a room at the Plaza Hotel. The heat exacerbates the tension in the air, and Tom begins to aggressively question Gatsby about his past. Tom then snaps and yells at Daisy, "I suppose the latest thing is to sit back and let Mr. Nobody from Nowhere make love to your wife." Gatsby responds by telling Tom that Daisy never loved him, and attempts to get Daisy to agree. Daisy, panic-stricken, tells Gatsby that she did love Tom once, but that she loved him also. Tom, who has looked into Gatsby, accuses him of illegal dealings with Wolfshiem, including bootlegging. Gatsby tries to defend himself to Daisy, not realizing that his dream is already dead.

On the way back from New York, Daisy drives Gatsby's car. Myrtle runs toward them, thinking Tom is driving, and Daisy accidentally hits and kills her. They leave the scene before Tom, Nick, and Jordan arrive. When Tom discovers what happened, he assumes Gatsby was driving. After Tom assures a distraught George Wilson that it was not his car, they leave and return to the Buchanan mansion. Nick refuses to go inside, disgusted with all of them. While waiting outside for a taxi, he sees Gatsby standing watch in the darkness. He tells Nick that it was Daisy who was driving, and that he needs to stay to make sure Tom does not hurt her. Gatsby is still clinging to his dream, and Nick leaves him alone in the dark, "watching over nothing."

Gatsby returns to West Egg in the early morning hours. With his façade shattered, he tells Nick the story of Dan Cody and of his courtship of Daisy. She represented everything that he had yearned for since he first caught sight of Dan Cody's yacht, and his dream of success took the shape of his love for her. For the first time, Gatsby starts to realize that Daisy may have loved Tom, though he insists that she always loved him more. When Nick leaves in the morning, he tells Gatsby: "They're a rotten crowd … You're worth the whole damn bunch put together"—the last words Nick would ever say to Gatsby, and the only compliment he ever gave him.

Nick interrupts the narrative to piece together the events that occurred at Wilson's garage that afternoon: Wilson slowly pieces together what had happened to Myrtle, and heads to Gatsby's mansion. There he finds Gatsby in the pool, waiting for a call from Daisy that would never come. It is at this point—Gatsby's lowest—that George Wilson shoots him and then kills himself, and with that "the holocaust is complete." With Myrtle, George, and Gatsby all dead, the novel's lower class has been wiped out.

When he learns of Gatsby's death, Nick calls Daisy, but finds that the Buchanans have left town. Gatsby's father arrives, and he shares stories of Gatsby's childhood with Nick. Mr. Gatz is proud of his son's accomplishments, not knowing how he really made his money. He shows Nick a schedule that Gatsby had written for himself when he was just a boy, detailing ways to better himself. Only Nick, Mr. Gatz, the servants, and Owl Eyes are in attendance at Gatsby's funeral.

After Gatsby's death, Nick breaks things off with Jordan. Bumping into Tom in New York, he discovers that Tom told Wilson that Gatsby killed Myrtle. Tom still does not know that it was Daisy that actually killed her, and although Nick despises him, he can't bring himself to tell Tom the truth. At this point, Nick sees the Buchanans for what they are:

> They were careless people, Tom and Daisy—they smashed up things and creatures and then retreated back into their money or their vast carelessness or whatever it was that kept them together, and let other people clean up the mess they had made.

Nick says goodbye to Tom and the East forever, and prepares to return home, taking one last look at Gatsby's "huge incoherent failure of a house."

For Gatsby, the dream of Daisy was the dream of something lost long ago, if it ever existed at all. His inability to accept that he could not recapture the past made his dream impossible, and he spent his life in a futile struggle against the inevitable

Harlem's Cotton Club was a popular jazz nightclub and speakeasy during the Prohibition era. The clientele was restricted to white patrons, even though many of the performers were African American.

progression of time. The final realization that he could not repeat the past is what killed Gatsby, just as much as the bullet from George Wilson's gun.

Cultural Context

Written during the height of the boom times of the 1920s, *The Great Gatsby* is inextricably linked with its time and place. With all the wealth of Wall Street, as well as jazz clubs and speakeasies, urban New York represented the shift from traditional values toward the modern culture of materialism and moral decline. This new American Dream appeared ripe for the taking in New York, but the traditionally wealthy American aristocracy looked down on the newly rich,

Many of the growing number of immigrants to America in the early twentieth century settled in crowded tenement houses such as this one, on New York City's Lower East Side.

who often made their money through illegal bootlegging or criminal stock transactions.

After World War I, many young men returned to a changed nation, and the ideals they had fought for overseas were being replaced by new values. After the horrors they had experienced, a generation sought happiness in the wild excesses of the modern world, but grew cynical and disillusioned as the honorable goals of freedom and democracy turned into the pursuit of wealth and excess.

Fitzgerald was in many ways a social historian. In *The Great Gatsby*, he is able to capture the mood of a nation at the height of prosperity, as well as the cultural changes taking place with the onset of Prohibition and the rise of consumer culture. He depicts the glamorous lifestyle of the rich, and material wealth in the form of luxurious mansions and flashy cars, but at the same time presents the other side of America—the criminal element, the working class, and the desperation of the poor to achieve success.

Major Characters

Jay Gatsby

Gatsby is the novel's title character and its tragic hero. Born James Gatz in North Dakota, he dreamed of becoming wealthy and successful. At age seventeen, when he saw Dan Cody's yacht, he transformed himself into Jay Gatsby and started the relentless pursuit of wealth that would continue for the rest of his life. When he meets and falls in love with Daisy Fay before the war, all his dreams of wealth and success manifest in her, and when he loses her to a rich man he turns to criminal activity to make the fortune he thinks will win her back. He buys a large mansion across the bay from hers, throws lavish parties, and buys luxurious cars and clothes, all with the singular goal of reclaiming Daisy. Ultimately, Gatsby's immense capacity for hope and the pursuit of his dream are what destroy him, as even after Daisy proves herself unworthy, he continues to believe he can repeat the past and make his dream of her into reality.

Nick Carraway

Nick is both a player in the story and its narrator. Though he comes from money, he retains the traditional American values of the Midwest: he is honest and has strong morals. He is the novel's moral compass and he often finds himself conflicted, demonstrating the effects of the modern world on traditional American values. This inner conflict is apparent in his relationship with Jordan Baker: he is attracted to her beauty and sophistication but disgusted by her dishonesty and carelessness. As the story progresses, Nick grows cynical and passes judgment on everyone around him. He realizes that the glitz and glamour of the East are a disguise for its emptiness and immorality and that the American Dream is a lie. Nick returns home to the West where he can live a quiet life based in traditional values. Nick is Fitzgerald's voice in the novel and expresses his belief that the pursuit of material wealth in the Jazz Age, while tempting, is a corrupt and damaging influence.

Daisy Buchanan

Daisy is the object of Gatsby's romantic quest. When she was an eighteen-year-old debutante in Louisville, Kentucky, Daisy met Gatsby, a lieutenant in the army stationed nearby. She fell in love with Gatsby, who lied about being from a wealthy family, but even though she promised to wait for him, she grew restless and married Tom Buchanan, a wealthy young man from a prominent Chicago family. Gatsby sees Daisy as representative of everything he has always wanted: she is beautiful, rich, charming, sophisticated, and aristocratic. She is the embodiment of wealth, and her "voice is full of money." But the reality of Daisy falls far short of Gatsby's dream of

The "Gatsby Cluster"

Between 1922 and 1924, Fitzgerald wrote a number of short stories in which he explored characters and themes he would later perfect in *The Great Gatsby*. These five stories, known as the "Gatsby Cluster," demonstrate the way in which Fitzgerald used his short story writing not just for fast money but also as a workshop for his novels. The stories included in the Gatsby cluster are: "The Diamond as Big as the Ritz" (June 1922); "Winter Dreams" (December 1922); "Dice, Brass Knuckles & Guitar" (May 1923); "Absolution" (June 1924); and "The Sensible Thing" (July 1924). Of these five stories, "Winter Dreams" and "Absolution" are the most closely associated with *The Great Gatsby*. "Absolution" was originally part of an early draft of the novel, in which Fitzgerald included the childhood of the character who would become Gatsby. "Winter Dreams" is essentially an early draft of the novel in short form, with the characters of Dexter Green and Judy Jones serving as preliminary sketches for Gatsby and Daisy.

her: she is shallow, careless, insincere, and values only money and the easy life it can provide. Her affair with Gatsby is less about love than it is about curing her constant boredom and restlessness. Daisy is both the reason for Gatsby's success and the cause of his downfall, and she represents the destructive, empty nature of wealth in modern America. The character of Daisy is loosely based on Zelda Fitzgerald and Ginevra King.

Tom Buchanan

Tom is, in every sense of the word, a powerful man. He comes from an aristocratic and incredibly wealthy Midwestern family, was a star football and polo player, and has an imposing physique and an aggressive, arrogant way about him. Tom is a hypocrite who bemoans the loss of traditional family values and morality in America while keeping an apartment for his mistress in New York. He is a cruel man who treats people like objects that he can use and abuse, going so far as to break Myrtle's nose simply for saying Daisy's name. Tom has no real affection for Daisy, whom he has been unfaithful to throughout their marriage, and only shows interest in keeping her when he is threatened by another man. Tom is the harsh reality of the wealth and prominence that Gatsby idealizes. His breeding and money give him the liberty to do whatever he wants without consequence.

Jordan Baker

Jordan is a professional golfer who grew up in Louisville with Daisy. She is a modern woman in many ways. Physically, she has the **androgynous** body type preferred by the New Woman: "a slender, small-breasted girl with an erect carriage … like a young cadet" who wore her dresses "like sports clothes." She is also the only female character in the novel that has her own identity and is not dependent on men. Jordan is also dishonest and lies "in order to keep that cool insolent smile turned to the world and yet satisfy the demands of her hard jaunty body."

While she is in many ways different from Daisy, she is equally as careless and morally corrupt as a result of her wealth and privilege.

Myrtle Wilson

Myrtle is the working-class mistress of Tom Buchanan. Though she is not beautiful, she has a sensuousness and vitality about her that attracts Tom. The wife of a poor garage owner, Myrtle enjoys the money and lifestyle that Tom provides for her. Despite the airs she puts on in her New York apartment, she is vulgar and low class. Myrtle's desire for wealth and a higher social status destroys her when she runs toward Gatsby's car, thinking it belongs to Tom, and is killed by Daisy in a hit-and-run accident.

Major Theme: The American Dream

Gatsby's dream mirrors the American Dream of the Jazz Age: to rise up from nothing and achieve success in the form of wealth and a glamorous lifestyle. It was, in many ways, an impossible dream for the majority of Americans in the 1920s. Despite the "get rich quick" mentality of the time, the truly wealthy were born that way, and those who did become rich during the boom times were not considered of the same class or status as those with "old money." Money, in truth, could not buy happiness, and the pursuit of wealth often led to corruption and illegal activity. Gatsby's story is America's story, and while the novel was written years before the Wall Street Crash of 1929, the death of Gatsby's dream—and of Gatsby himself—predicted the future of an America built on the illusion that "Coolidge Prosperity" would last forever.

Fitzgerald represents the differences between traditional wealth and new money in the towns of East Egg and West Egg. Though physically the same and separated only by a bay, the two are worlds apart. East Eggers look down on West

Eggers, and nowhere is this more evident than when the two worlds collide at Gatsby's parties. When Daisy and Tom—the embodiment of East Egg old money—attend Gatsby's party, Daisy is "appalled by West Egg" and sees "something awful in the very simplicity she failed to understand." Tom, also repulsed by the spectacle of the party, speculates that Gatsby is a bootlegger, as "a lot of these newly rich people are."

The difference is also apparent in material possessions. Gatsby's mansion is described as a replica of a French hotel, while the Buchanan mansion is described in terms that physically root it to the land—an example of the way in which the people of East Egg are established, and those from West Egg are imitations transplanted from somewhere else. Despite all Gatsby's attempts to emulate the wealth that Daisy values— the huge mansion, the lavish parties, the luxurious clothes and cars—he will always be an imposter.

There is very little religious imagery in the novel, which reflects the trend of secularization in Jazz Age America. Faith in God was replaced by faith in material things, and this is apparent in the eyes of Doctor T. J. Eckleburg. The only religious character in the novel, George Wilson looks out at the billboard and tells his neighbor, Michaelis, that "God sees everything," to which Michaelis replies, "That's an advertisement." That the only explicit representation of God in the novel is an advertisement is significant, as is the fact that the only character that sees God at all is the impoverished Wilson. The only other religious image is presented in Gatsby's pursuit of Daisy, which is compared to "the following of a **grail**." The quest for the grail (a plate or cup used by Jesus Christ at the Last Supper) is traditionally a religious quest, but Gatsby's grail is Daisy, and his quest is the pursuit of the wealth she represents. In the modern world, God is mostly absent, and the material has replaced the spiritual.

In the novel's **coda**, Nick reflects on the American Dream, viewing the land through the eyes of the first Dutch sailor to see the new world. Fitzgerald demonstrates the futility of the new American Dream when he compares the discovery of the "green breast of the new world" to the green light at the end of Daisy's dock. The first colonists viewed the new world as a land of endless opportunity and freedom—"the last and greatest of all human dreams." Much like Gatsby seeing the green light at the end of Daisy's dock for the first time, the Dutch sailor "must have held his breath in the presence of this continent … face to face for the last time in history with something commensurate to his capacity for wonder." However, in the modern world of the Jazz Age, the American Dream has been corrupted, and if it still exists anywhere, it is far outside the city. Gatsby's pursuit of this impossible dream killed him, and Nick only escapes this fate by returning to the Midwest, where traditional values have not yet been corrupted by the modern world.

Major Symbols

Automobiles

Automobiles were a major symbol of wealth and status in the Jazz Age, and in *The Great Gatsby*, the kind of car characters drive says a lot about them. Nick describes Gatsby's car as "a rich cream color, bright with nickel, swollen here and there in its monstrous length." Only Nick describes it as cream; for the rest of the novel, it is referred to as yellow. As opposed to Tom's more muted blue coupé, Gatsby's yellow "circus wagon" is an ostentatious display of wealth characteristic of the newly moneyed class. Though he does own a car, Tom prefers horses, which represent the traditional American form of transportation and symbolizes the Buchanan family's aristocratic roots. There is a "dust-covered wreck of a Ford" in George Wilson's garage for repair, which symbolizes the type of car that was affordable to the working class and stands in sharp contrast to the bright, shiny cars driven by the wealthy. Most significantly, Myrtle is killed by Gatsby's car (a symbol of a failed attempt to emulate traditional wealth) while Daisy, who represents traditional wealth, is driving. Both Gatsby and Myrtle, who in different ways tried and failed to elevate their position in society, are killed as a result of Daisy's accident, and this is symbolic of the corrupting influence of wealth on people who pursue it.

The Valley of Ashes

In the valley of ashes, Fitzgerald shows the bleak, harsh reality of 1920s America. Inspired in part by T.S. Eliot's poem "The Waste Land" (1922), the valley of ashes symbolizes the moral decay and destruction of the world as a result of modernity and industrialization. It is the literal dumping ground for the products of New York's industry and capitalism, and those who live and work there have no chance at the upward mobility promised by the American Dream. George Wilson fixes cars, but cannot afford one. Myrtle Wilson tries to rise up through adultery, sacrificing her morals for material wealth, and it kills her.

Wealthy people commuting to and from New York are just passing through, and when the train stops briefly at the station there, "the ash-grey men swarm up with leaden spades and stir up an impenetrable cloud which screens their obscure operations from … sight." The working-class people are literally invisible to the upper class. The valley is also home to many immigrants: Wilson's neighbor, Michaelis, is Greek, and when Tom sees "a grey, scrawny Italian child … setting torpedoes in a row along the railroad track" he remarks to Nick, "Terrible place isn't it." In the 1920s, Americans associated the immigrant population with poverty and corruption, and they were discriminated against and forced to take low-paying jobs.

A young woman poses with a luxurious 1927 Lincoln L-series town car outside a stage door in Hollywood, California.

The Green Light

The green light symbolizes both Gatsby's dream of Daisy and the American Dream, both of which seemed to be just within reach but proved impossible to get. For Gatsby, the green light represents the "orgastic future" of a happy life with Daisy, and all the wealth and success that came with her. But Gatsby's dream of Daisy is also a dream of the past, and the dream "recedes year by year" before him. Gatsby's idealized version of Daisy no longer exists; she has been corrupted by her wealth, just as the American Dream of happiness was corrupted by the wealth and materialism of the Jazz Age. Society was in a state of moral decay, with people turning to criminal activity to get rich quick and indulging in excessive drinking and consumption of material goods for entertainment. But Gatsby had "an extraordinary gift for hope" and "a romantic readiness" that allowed him to believe he could repeat the past, and the green light symbolizes all his hopes and dreams for an impossible future.

Timeline

1896 Francis Scott Key Fitzgerald born September 24 in St. Paul, Minnesota, to Edward Fitzgerald and Mollie McQuillan Fitzgerald.

1900 Zelda Sayre born July 24 in Montgomery, Alabama.

1908 Henry Ford introduces the Model T.

1912 Fitzgerald meets Father Sigourney Fay.

1913 Fitzgerald enters Princeton University. Woodrow Wilson takes office as 28th President of the United States.

1914 World War I begins in Europe.

1915 Fitzgerald meets Ginevra King.

1917 U.S. enters World War I on April 6. Fitzgerald commissioned as second lieutenant in the U.S. Army. Reports to Fort Leavenworth, Kansas, for training. Begins *The Romantic Egotist*. Bolsheviks overthrow Russian government in October Revolution.

1918 Fitzgerald reports to Camp Sheridan near Montgomery, Alabama. Meets Zelda. Scribner's rejects *The Romantic Egotist*. Armistice declared on November 11.

1919 18th Amendment is ratified. Fitzgerald discharged from the army and moves to New York to work at an advertising agency. Zelda breaks their engagement. Treaty of Versailles signed on June 28, officially ending World War I. Wartime Prohibition Act goes into effect on July 1 and Prohibition begins. Scribner's accepts *This Side of Paradise*.

1920 18th Amendment goes into effect on January 16. *This Side of Paradise* is published. Fitzgerald and Zelda marry. Revival of the Ku Klux Klan. First commercial radio broadcast. 19th Amendment ratified, giving women the right to vote.

1921 Warren G. Harding takes office as 29th President of the United States. Emergency Immigration Act is passed, restricting immigration to the United States. Scottie Fitzgerald born October 26.

1922 *The Beautiful and Damned* is published. Fitzgeralds move to Great Neck.

1923 Harding dies and Vice President Calvin Coolidge takes office as 30th President of the United States.

1924 Fitzgeralds move to France. Zelda begins relationship with Edouard Jozan. Fitzgerald writes *The Great Gatsby*. Johnson-Reed Act further restricts immigration.

Timeline

1925 *The Great Gatsby* is published. Fitzgerald meets Ernest Hemingway. KKK marches on Washington, D.C.

1927 Fitzgerald takes first job in Hollywood. Charles Lindbergh completes first solo transatlantic flight. Babe Ruth breaks home run record. *The Jazz Singer* becomes first full-length talking picture.

1928 Fitzgeralds return to Paris. Zelda begins ballet lessons with Lubov Egorova. Fitzgeralds return to America.

1929 Herbert Hoover takes office as 31st President of the United States. Stock Market Crash on October 29 ushers in the Great Depression.

1930 Zelda has her first breakdown and is institutionalized at Malmaison Clinic in Paris. Enters Prangins clinic in Switzerland.

1931 Death of Edward Fitzgerald. Zelda released from Prangins and the Fitzgeralds return to America. Fitzgerald takes second job in Hollywood. Death of Judge Sayre. Francis Scott Key's "The Star-Spangled Banner" becomes the national anthem.

1932 Zelda suffers second breakdown and is institutionalized at Phipps Clinic in Baltimore.

1933 21st Amendment repeals Prohibition. Franklin Delano Roosevelt takes office as 32nd President of the United States.

1934 Zelda suffers third breakdown and enters Sheppard-Pratt Hospital near Baltimore. *Tender Is the Night* is published.

1935 Fitzgerald moves to North Carolina and writes "The Crack-Up" essays.

1936 *Esquire* publishes "The Crack-Up" essays. Zelda enters Highland Hospital in Asheville, North Carolina. Death of Mollie McQuillan Fitzgerald.

1937 Fitzgerald returns to Hollywood and meets Sheilah Graham.

1939 Fitzgerald travels to Cuba with Zelda and goes on alcoholic binge. Begins work on *The Last Tycoon*. World War II begins in Europe.

1940 Fitzgerald dies of a heart attack on December 21 in Hollywood, California.

1941 *The Last Tycoon* is published. U.S. enters World War II.

1945 *The Crack-Up* is published. U.S. drops atomic bombs on Hiroshima and Nagasaki, Japan. World War II ends in Allied victory.

Fitzgerald's Most Important Works

Novels
This Side of Paradise (1920)
The Beautiful and Damned (1922)
The Great Gatsby (1925)
Tender Is the Night (1934)
The Last Tycoon (1941)

Short Story Collections
Flappers and Philosophers (1920)
Tales of the Jazz Age (1922)
All the Sad Young Men (1926)
Taps at Reveille (1935)
The Short Stories of F. Scott Fitzgerald (1989),
    ed. Matthew J. Bruccoli

Short Stories
"Babes in the Woods" (1919)
"Bernice Bobs Her Hair" (1920)
"May Day" (1920)
"Winter Dreams" (1922)
"Absolution" (1924)
"Babylon Revisited" (1931)

Essay Collections

The Crack-Up (1941), ed. Edmund Wilson
A Short Autobiography (2011), ed. James L.W. West III

Essays

"Echoes of the Jazz Age" (1931)
"My Lost City" (1932)
"The Crack-Up" (1936)
"Early Success" (1937)

Glossary

androgynous
Being neither distinguishably masculine nor feminine, as in dress, appearance, or behavior.

Bolsheviks
A radical faction of the Russian Social Democratic Party who represented the working class and used revolutionary tactics to seize state power by force.

bootlegging
Making, selling, and/or transporting illegal alcohol for sale.

coda
An ending part of a piece of music or a work of literature or drama that is separate from the earlier parts.

communist
An individual or political party believing in a system of government in which the state plans and controls the economy and a single, often authoritarian party holds power, claiming to make progress toward a higher social order in which all goods are equally shared by the people.

egotist
A conceited, self-absorbed individual who believes that he or she is better, more important, and/or more talented than other people.

flappers
Young women in the 1920s who rejected conventional feminine appearance, dress, and behavior.

grail
In medieval legend, the cup or platter used by Jesus Christ at the Last Supper, and in which Joseph of Arimathea received Christ's blood at the Cross.

idealism
The attitude of a person who believes that it is possible to live according to very high standards of behavior and honesty.

laissez-faire
An economic policy that allows businesses to operate with very little interference from the government.

margin call
A demand by a broker that an investor deposit more money to cover possible losses.

nativism
A sociopolitical policy favoring the interests of native inhabitants over those of immigrants, often accompanied by prejudice against new inhabitants by the native population.

Glossary

parochial
A type of private school that is run by a church parish.

progressive
A person or party advocating moderate political change and reform, especially social improvement by governmental action.

Prohibition
The prevention by law of the manufacture, transport, and sale of alcoholic beverages.

propaganda
Ideas or statements that are often false or exaggerated and that are spread in order to help a cause, political leader, or government.

protagonist
The leading character, hero, or heroine of a drama or other literary work.

recession
A period of decline in activity across the economy, lasting longer than a few months, that affects industrial production, employment, income, and trade.

schizophrenia
A very serious mental illness in which someone cannot think or behave normally and often experiences delusions.

speakeasies
Establishments, especially nightclubs, for the illegal sale and consumption of alcoholic beverages.

Sources

Introduction

P. 7: Bruccoli, Matthew J., Scottie Fitzgerald Smith, and Joan P. Kerr, eds., *The Romantic Egoists* (Columbia, SC: University of South Carolina Press, 2003), 240.

Chapter 1

P. 12: Harding, Warren G., Campaign Speech in Boston, Massachusetts, May 14, 1920, <teachingamericanhistory.org/library/document/return-to-normalcy> (accessed December 17, 2013).

P. 13: Coolidge, Calvin, "The Press Under a Free Government," January 17, 1925, <www.calvin-coolidge.org/press-under-free-government> (accessed December 17, 2013).

P. 27: Miller, Nathan, *New World Coming: The 1920s and the Making of Modern America* (Cambridge, MA: Da Capo Press, 2003), 359.

P. 29: Fitzgerald, F. Scott, "Echoes of The Jazz Age," in *The Crack-Up*, ed. Edmund Wilson (New York: New Directions, 1945), 21.

Chapter 2

P. 35: Fitzgerald, F. Scott, *This Side of Paradise* (New York: Dover, 1996), 25.

P. 40: Fitzgerald, F. Scott, "My Lost City," in *The Crack-Up*, ed. Edmund Wilson (New York: New Directions, 1945), 26.

P. 43: Fitzgerald, F. Scott, "Early Success," in *The Crack-Up*, ed. Edmund Wilson (New York: New Directions, 1945), 89.

P. 50: Fitzgerald, F. Scott, "The Crack-Up," in *The Crack-Up*, ed. Edmund Wilson (New York: New Directions, 1945), 72.

Chapter 3

All quotations from *This Side of Paradise* are from the 1996 Dover edition.

Chapter 4

All quotations from *The Great Gatsby* are from the 2003 Scribner edition.

Further Information

Books

Boon, Kevin Alexander. *F. Scott Fitzgerald*. New York, NY: Marshall Cavendish Benchmark, 2006.

Currell, Susan. *American Culture in the 1920s*. (Twentieth-Century American Culture series) Edinburgh, Scotland: Edinburgh University Press, 2009.

Drowne, Kathleen, and Patrick Huber. *The 1920s*. (American Popular Culture Through History series) Westport, CT: Greenwood, 2004.

Pelzer, Linda C. *Student Companion to F. Scott Fitzgerald*. Westport, CT: Greenwood Press, 2000.

Websites

Digital History: 1920s
www.digitalhistory.uh.edu/era.cfm?eraID=13&smtID=2

The F. Scott Fitzgerald Society
www.fscottfitzgeraldsociety.org/index.html

History.com: The Roaring Twenties
www.history.com/topics/roaring-twenties

Bibliography

Boon, Kevin Alexander. *F. Scott Fitzgerald.*
New York, NY: Marshall Cavendish Benchmark, 2006.

Bruccoli, Matthew J. *Some Sort of Epic Grandeur: The Life of F. Scott Fitzgerald.* Second Revised Edition. Columbia, SC: University of South Carolina Press, 2002.

Bruccoli, Matthew J., ed. *F. Scott Fitzgerald: A Life in Letters.* New York: Charles Scribner's Sons, 1994.

Bruccoli, Matthew J., and Jackson R. Bryer, eds. *F. Scott Fitzgerald in His Own Time: A Miscellany.* Kent, OH: Kent State University Press, 1971.

Bruccoli, Matthew J., Scottie Fitzgerald Smith, and Joan P. Kerr, eds. *The Romantic Egoists.* Columbia, SC: University of South Carolina Press, 2003.

Currell, Susan. *American Culture in the 1920s.* Edinburgh, Scotland: Edinburgh University Press, 2009.

Dumenil, Lynn. *The Modern Temper: American Culture and Society in the 1920s.* New York, NY: Hill and Wang, 1995.

Fitzgerald, F. Scott. *The Crack-Up.* (Edmund Wilson, ed.) New York, NY: New Directions, 1945.

Bibliography

Fitzgerald, F. Scott. *The Great Gatsby*. New York, NY: Charles Scribner's Sons, 1925.

Fitzgerald, F. Scott. *The Notebooks of F. Scott Fitzgerald*. New York, NY and London, England: Harcourt Brace Jovanovich/Bruccoli Clark, 1980.

Fitzgerald, F. Scott. *A Short Autobiography*. (James L.W. West III, ed.) New York, NY: Charles Scribner's Sons, 2011.

Fitzgerald, F. Scott. *The Short Stories of F. Scott Fitzgerald*. (Matthew J. Bruccoli, ed.) New York, NY: Charles Scribner's Sons, 1989.

Fitzgerald, F. Scott. *This Side of Paradise*. New York, NY: Dover, 1996.

Gale, Robert L. *An F. Scott Fitzgerald Encyclopedia*. Westport, CT: Greenwood Press, 1998.

Goldberg, David J. *Discontented America: The United States in the 1920s*. Baltimore: Johns Hopkins University Press, 1999.

Hearn, Charles R. "F. Scott Fitzgerald and the Popular Magazine Formula Story of the Twenties." *Journal of American Culture* 18, no. 3 (1995): 33.

Kyvig, David E. *Daily Life in the United States, 1920–1940.* Chicago: Ivan R. Dee, 2004.

Miller, Nathan. *New World Coming: The 1920s and the Making of Modern America.* Cambridge, MA: Da Capo Press, 2003.

Pelzer, Linda C. *Student Companion to F. Scott Fitzgerald.* Westport, CT: Greenwood Press, 2000.

Prigozy, Ruth, ed. *The Cambridge Companion to F. Scott Fitzgerald.* Cambridge: Cambridge University Press, 2002.

Rielly, Edward J. *F. Scott Fitzgerald: A Biography.* Westport, CT: Greenwood Press, 2005.

Shuman, R. Baird, ed. *Great American Writers: Twentieth Century.* New York, NY: Marshall Cavendish, 2002.

Tate, Mary Jo. *F. Scott Fitzgerald A to Z.* New York, NY: Checkmark Books, 1998.

Index

About the Author

Alison Morretta holds a Bachelor of Arts in English and Creative Writing from Kenyon College in Gambier, Ohio, where she studied the history and literature of the Jazz Age. She has worked in book publishing since 2005, developing and copyediting both fiction and nonfiction manuscripts. Alison lives in New York City with her loving husband, Bart, and their rambunctious Corgi, Cassidy. In addition to this title, Alison penned two other books in this series, *John Steinbeck and the Great Depression* and *Harriet Beecher Stowe and the Abolitionist Movement.*